D0077123

Managing
Global Operations

Managing Global Operations

Cultural and Technical Success Factors

Scott T. Young and
Winter Nie

Quorum Books
Westport, Connecticut • London

Library of Congress Cataloging-in-Publication Data

Young, Scott T.
    Managing global operations : cultural and technical success factors /
Scott T. Young, Winter Nie.
        p. cm.
    Includes bibliographical references and index.
    ISBN 0–89930–870–8 (alk. paper)
    1. International business enterprises—Management. I. Nie, Winter.
II. Title.
HD62.4.Y678   1996   95–26267
658'.049—dc20

British Library Cataloguing in Publication Data is available.

Copyright © 1996 by Scott T. Young and Winter Nie

All rights reserved. No portion of this book may be
reproduced, by any process or technique, without the
express written consent of the publisher.

Library of Congress Catalog Card Number: 95-26267
ISBN: 0–89930–870–8

First published in 1996

Quorum Books, 88 Post Road West, Westport, CT 06881
An imprint of Greenwood Publishing Group, Inc.

Printed in the United States of America

∞™

The paper used in this book complies with the
Permanent Paper Standard issued by the National
Information Standards Organization (Z39.48–1984).

10 9 8 7 6 5 4 3 2 1

To Thomas and Grace Young,
Teresa, and Jim and Aspen.

Contents

Tables and Figures

Acknowledgments

We would like to express our appreciation to our respective universities, the University of Utah and Colorado State University, for their support in this endeavor. The Center for International Business Education and Research of the University of Utah and Brigham Young University, led by James Gardner, Brooklyn Derr, and Lee Radebaugh, was a valuable resource for this work. Editors Marcy Winer and James Ice were very helpful in making many constructive suggestions. A number of individuals contributed greatly to the research that went into this book. These include Jim Faryar, Duane Byrge, Darrell Brown, Mary and Dr. William Lanier, Lucia and John Geraci, Pam and Rich Marks, Robert Wilken, Richard Wilken, Joyce Bardin, Ronald Young, Deanna Froerer, David Dyches, Sharon and Thomas W. Young, Cathy and Nelson Siso, Sue Parker, Mark LeKing, Stefan Foskey, Jeffrey Foskey, Francis and Junior Foskey, Robert B. Young, and Suzanne Robinson.

Also, many thanks to Sharon Lee and Annamarie Shotwell for their assistance, and Dean John Seybolt for his guidance.

Managing Global Operations: An Overview

Many business books begin with a perfunctory statement similar to "In these turbulent, dynamic, complex, days of global management. . . . " We believe that firms doing business across the globe have communications tools that make global management infinitely easier in the 1990s than in prior decades. Fax machines, E-mail, satellite communications, cellular telephones, and computer local area networks are tools that enable managers to communicate at speeds few could have imagined a short time ago. We have never had it easier. Certainly there has been much political turmoil in the 1990s: the crumbling of the Eastern bloc, wars in the Middle East and Bosnia, racial strife in South Africa—but such turbulence is not peculiar to modern times. What we do have today is the ability to spot political trends faster. Through satellite communications, we receive vital news reports and coverage at speeds never before available.

Those who insist that the management of the global firm is more difficult in 1996 are correct in that decisions must be made faster, and operations must be quick to change directions in order to survive. Business trends shift as quickly in the 1990s as the technologies that tell us about the shifts.

This book focuses on the operations management of the global firm. The operations function includes such activities as forecasting production, scheduling of labor and production, total quality management, productivity management, facility layout and location, materials management, purchasing, and incoming and outgoing logistics. A proper definition of a "global" firm is one in which a majority of sales is through exports. We use the term more broadly, to include all firms that have foreign sales.

The operations function is at the very soul of the organization. The function is made up of men and women who are responsible for production. Because of their intimacy with the product, the people of production know more than anyone else in the organization about what goes into that product.

We address the needs of both global manufacturing and global service firms. Each has its own peculiar set of problems to be examined. Operations management in service firms include similar activities to manufacturing firms, although the final product may be less tangible in the service firm.

The book is organized into thirteen additional chapters: Chapter 2, A Roadmap to Global Operations, establishes the rules of the game for global operations and presents the major questions facing operations managers today. Chapter 3, Global Operations Strategy, shows the operations function provides competitive advantage for the global firm. The strategies of human resources, quality, production planning and control, technology management, facilities location and layout, vertical integration, and speed are employed to gain advantage and strive for profitability. Chapter 4, Managing Productivity and Quality, gives advice on mastering the challenge of maintaining uniform quality and productivity programs in multiple locations across the world. Chapter 5, Materials Management and Sourcing, reviews important inventory considerations. Topics include just-in-time inventory systems, materials resources planning, and distribution requirements planning. Chapter 6, Facility Location and Layout, tells us where to build a plant, headquarters, or regional office. The facilities location decision encompasses a number of key variables, including financial incentives, cost considerations, transportation, access to markets, availability and skill level of labor, access to materials, and site availability. These decisions must anticipate market changes, and product and process life cycles.

Within the plant, layout decisions are critical to building an efficient production system. Plant size and focus are also considered. Chapter 7, Managing Human Resources in Global Operations, explores the people skills aspect of operations. The biggest factor in effective operations management is the ability of the work force. Dealing with multiple cultures, managers must train and motivate workers to attain high levels of skill, knowledge, and commitment. Chapter 8, Cultural Impact on Operations, reviews cultural issues that must be headed. Much of the success or failure of international production can be attributed to cultural factors. Chapter 9, Effective Global Project Management, offers a "How-to" for global project management and scheduling. Key managerial issues and success factors are reviewed. Chapter 10, Technology

Management for Global Operations, reviews key issues for the management of operations technology. Chapter 11, Managing International Service Operations, presents many of the issues pertinent to service operations. These issues are uniquely different from manufacturing organizations. Chapter 12, Coordination, discusses operations' relationship with marketing, research and development, and cost accounting and reviews a number of coordination mechanisms to improve this process. Chapter 13, Human-Centered Production, presents a new concept—focusing operations efforts on the human element.

Chapter 14, Conclusion, summarizes the issues presented in the preceding chapters.

This book is intended to serve as a handbook for practicing managers involved or interested in the operations management of global firms. It is aimed at managers practicing global operations and at managers interfacing with operations and attempting to understand the demands of operations.

A Road Map to Global Operations

The initial decision to globalize an organization requires a great deal of planning and consideration. Which country in that region should the company make its first overtures to? Which city in the country has the best location? What form of global operations should the company adopt? These are some of the big questions that any company intending to globalize its operations must answer. At the initial deliberation stage, other operational factors such as location, capacity, human resources, materials management, and technology come into play.

From a macro perspective, the foreign country's political climate, legal systems, government regulations, and economic status will inevitably impact the business environment. At the micro level, local tax treaties, availability of skilled labor, infrastructure of the city, transportation, proximity to raw materials, wage structure, and quality of life can impact day-to-day operations. Multifactors such as culture, religion, customs, natural resources, attitude of local people towards foreign investment, and openness of the community all have a significant bearing on shaping the future success of the global operations.

In this chapter, we will discuss forces that drive global operations, basic forms of global operations, and finally, a road map to global operations.

FACTORS FOR GLOBAL OPERATIONS

Sheth and Eshghi (1992) offer four factors that motivate companies to contemplate the use of global operations: cost competitiveness, competitive markets, manufacturing processes, and government policy.

Cost competitiveness. Two popular generic strategies are cost leadership and differentiation. The cost leadership strategy seeks to achieve and maintain a competitive advantage through realizing lower unit costs of production and distribution. The differentiation strategy attempts to achieve a competitive advantage through providing features that differentiate the product or service.

Competitive markets. Time-based competition mandates that the faster the company reacts to market changes, the quicker it brings its products to the market, the more likely the company is to survive and succeed. Advantages derive from being close to the local market: The company is quick to bring its products to the local market—some products have a short shelf life and shipping via air is usually too costly; consumers are more sophisticated in choosing products and services, and tastes change rapidly—being close to the local market not only enables the company to customize its products to local flavors but also allows it to be more responsive to market changes.

When the domestic market shows signs of approaching maturity, expanding to an overseas market can be a significant step toward seeking continued growth. When Nike decided to open a plant in China, important considerations included not only the cheap labor and materials costs but also the enormous market potential that China presents. The prospect of capturing one percent of China's total population of 1.2 billion people would translate into over ten million pairs of shoes for Nike. However, it does not take long before an untapped market is flooded with competition.

Manufacturing competency. Flexible manufacturing, JIT, CAD, and CAM make globalizing operations feasible. The increasing use of information technology in manufacturing and services improves global networks, reduces long-distance barriers, and shortens the communication time. Several U.S. credit-card companies and banks own data-processing facilities in Latin American and Asian countries to take advantage of the low labor costs. This way, outcomes from on-the-spot processing are communicated back through information networks almost instantaneously. Without jeopardizing the quality of service and responsiveness to customers, they are able to reduce data-processing costs.

Manufacturing competency is closely related to technology. Technology (hard and soft) costs often make globalizing operations necessary because of the large amount of capital investment required, something a small domestic market may not be able to fund. For instance, McDonalds can be found in most major cities of the world. The standard equipment and expertise makes the transfer of technology borderless.

An important factor in manufacturing competency is the exchange of technology across national boundaries. To compete on a global basis, Ford not only transfers technology to foreign countries but also tries to learn from locals. The exchange of ideas and expertise among people from various parts of the world serves to broaden perspectives and adds richness and variety to the knowledge base. This experience of exchanging, teaching, and relearning can be brought back to improve domestic manufacturing and is an important step towards achieving a world class manufacturing excellence.

Government policy. World economics require nations to have an open approach to companies seeking global operations. Even Communist countries like Vietnam and Cuba are considering opening their doors to outside investment. China and Russia have begun to privatize some industries that were traditionally controlled by government and considered as public sectors. This creates a tremendous opportunity for developed countries, considering the geographic size and population of China and Russia. China set up several economic development zones that provide tax breaks and other business incentives to attract foreign investment. For instance, TangGu, a special economic zone between Tianjing and Beijing has seen a healthy influx of foreign facilities. Outside of these "special zones," the Chinese government gives special tax treatment to joint ventures between domestic and foreign countries. The incentives are so lucrative that many domestic organizations, in the form of state-owned enterprises, collective enterprises, and private enterprises, are aggressively seeking joint ventures with foreign companies. Other countries such as Ireland, Mexico, Thailand, and Malaysia have provided similar economic incentives to attract foreign manufacturing to their countries.

FORMS OF GLOBAL OPERATIONS

Schroeder (1993) divides international firms into three categories. *Global firms* are characterized by marketing a similar product throughout the world, having an international network of coordinated sales and production facilities, and using a worldwide scale of operations and technology. *Multinational firms* produce and market products suited to local tastes and usually have independent foreign subsidiaries or divisions. *Export firms* produce in domestic facilities and ship to various foreign markets.

Sheth and Eshghi (1992) presented a similar framework based on capacity rationalization and localization of operations. Capacity rationalization refers to efficiency of operations. Localization of operations includes such issues as the technical standards in each country, government regulation, special characteristics of local markets, and international transportation costs.

When neither capacity rationalization nor localization of operations is important, *export operations* may be a good choice if the generic product would be acceptable to the local market, domestic facilities have enough capacity to accommodate export volume, and transportation cost is reasonable.

When both capacity rationalization and localization of operations are important, *multinational operations* could be adopted. Foreign subsidiaries can be set up so that products such as home electronic appliances can be made to cater to the local market. Karaoke sound systems are very popular in Asian countries, but a standard sound system without the sing-along feature may be a hard sell in these countries. A large volume refrigerator, well accepted in Western countries, may prove impractical in China because of the small living quarters and the tradition of buying fresh vegetables every morning.

When capacity rationalization is not important, *localized operations* in the form of licenses or joint ventures may be appropriate. Baby food manufacturing usually expands to its foreign market through joint ventures. Each country may have different health standards and labeling requirements for food products. Food is a very localized product. Local expertise in meeting government regulations and adapting food to the local market is necessary. The equipment, manufacturing process, and technology developed and used in domestic manufacturing plants can usually directly applied or transferred to joint ventures with few modifications. A foreign company can also license the technology or process to the local company to minimize direct investment.

When capacity rationalization is important and localization of operations is not important, *global operations* may be desirable. A company could have one manufacturing plant in France to serve the European market and one plant in Singapore to serve the Asian market. The company could have a plant in Hong Kong to produce one component, a plant in Seoul to produce another component, and a plant in Bangkok to perform the final assembly to serve the whole Asian market.

A ROAD MAP TO GLOBAL OPERATIONS

Globalizing operations is a strategic issue in that it impacts not only a firm's current business performances but also its survival and success in the future. There are many factors involved in deciding whether to globalize operations, when to proceed, which form of global operations to take, where to locate the global operations, and how to manage daily operations in a foreign country.

The first stage of global operations planning is to decide whether, and if so, when to globalize operations. The second stage is to decide the form of global operations and the location. The third stage involves detailed decision making regarding infrastructure, location, capacity, inventory management, technology, and human resources management.

Stage I. Globalizing Operations

There are many forces that drive companies to consider globalizing operations. This decision involves factors ranging from product, domestic market, cost, competition to manufacturing competency, foreign market, and other considerations.

Product
1. Does the product life cycle show signs of approaching maturity in the domestic market?
2. Is the product in demand in other countries?

When the product life cycle approaches maturity in the domestic market, it is often the time to explore international markets. For example, the demand for farming equipment has leveled off in the U.S., but developing countries have a great demand for the equipment. These countries have not acquired the necessary technology, expertise, and manufacturing capability to produce the equipment, so there is a great potential for globalizing operations.

Domestic Market
1. Does the market become increasingly competitive?
2. Is the profit margin squeezed due to competition?
3. Is the growth slowing down?

When the domestic market becomes increasingly competitive and the profit margin is being squeezed steadily, globalizing operations is usually a good choice to offset the slow growth in the domestic market. Ford and GM have reported sales increases in European and Asian markets in recent years while the sales in domestic market has been stagnant.

Cost
1. Is the labor cost increasing rapidly and, thus, squeezing the profit margin?

2. Is the materials cost increasing dramatically and hurting the financial performance?
3. Is it cheaper to acquire the materials from overseas?

In a saturated market, competition usually leads to cutting prices and offering better services. Both options erode the company's profit margin. Most canned pineapples sold in the United States used to come from the Hawaiian islands. More and more canned pineapples are shipped from Southeast Asia to the U.S. due to the cost difference. When there is a cost advantage in acquiring the materials from foreign countries, it provides an opportunity for importing, franchising, and establishing joint ventures.

Strategy and Competition
1. Are your competitors planning to move overseas or have they already moved overseas?
2. Is expanding into other countries one of the company's major goals?
3. Does the company want to be a leader or a follower in pursuing globalizing operations?
4. Is the company seeking an international market niche?

When competitors offer products of comparable quality with lower prices, this forces a response. Motorola saw a great market potential in China, and competitors from Hong Kong, Taiwan, and Korea moved into this untapped market; it immediately established a joint venture. Sometimes, the first entrant into a market captures the initial market share and builds customer loyalty, although there are risks associated with being the first into unfamiliar territories. A company may decide to wait and observe the success of the first entrant.

Manufacturing Competency
1. Does the company have extra capacity while the domestic market is quite mature?
2. Is the production process unique or standard?
3. Do companies in foreign countries offer other aspects of manufacturing competencies that the domestic company lacks?
4. Does technology require a large amount of investment?

When product demand in the domestic market has tapered off and the company has extra capacity, it is usually a good idea to think about expanding into international arenas. When the investment in technology is large and the domestic market is too small to justify the investment, expanding into global markets may be necessary to warrant the stake. When the production process is unique, there may be a market for licensing the technology in other countries.

Standard production processes make globalizing operations a little bit easier. McDonald's provides a good example. When companies in other countries can offer manufacturing competencies that the domestic firm lacks, joint ventures with these companies help the domestic company move towards world class manufacturing.

Foreign Market
1. Does the local government provide incentives for attracting foreign investment?
2. Is there a market potential for the product?
3. What is the buying power in that foreign market?

Government policy regarding foreign investment is usually a reliable indicator of a country's economic receptiveness. When exporting to a country constrained by factors such as government regulations and tariff barriers, building a subsidiary or joint venture may be the only way to reach the potential market. Two soft drink giants, Coca Cola and Pepsi, have recently entered the Chinese market. The market potential in China may be more than the U.S. market, considering a population of 1.2 billion people. Perhaps more important than the population in deciding the market size is purchasing power.

Other Considerations
1. Is it too risky to put all the investment in one country?
2. Can the company take advantage of exchange rate, inflation rate, and other volatile factors?

Other considerations such as diversifying investment and taking advantage of exchange rates can also prompt investors to venture into global operations. The volatility of these factors creates opportunities and speculations for some businesses

Stage II. Form of Global Operations

Once a company has decided to globalize, it must decide on the form and location of global operations. The firm may have various plans: to build a subsidiary in country A, to use a joint venture form in country B. Choosing the forms of global operations can be approached from product, capacity utilization, technology transfer, availability of materials and components, transportation cost, and other considerations. Deciding the locations of global operations can be based on an analysis of the destination nations' political, legal, and economic conditions.

Sheth and Eshghi (1992) proposed four forms of global operations (1992): Global operations, multinational operations, export operations, and localized operations, which include licenses and joint ventures.

Product
1. Is the localization of the product important?
2. Is the product generic?
3. Does the product have a preponderance of service elements?

A product such as a roll of color film is generic in the sense that the consumer requirement for its features and usage does not change from one country to another. The firm can produce a similar product in several countries using a coordinated network of production facilities and market it throughout the world. When the localization of the product is an important issue, multinational operations and localized operations are better choices. With localized operations, the firm is able to customize the product to the local flavor and respond more quickly to market changes.

Capacity Utilization
1. Is capacity utilization a critical issue?
2. Can the firm take advantage of possible economy of scale?

Automation requires a high initial investment. When capacity utilization is an important issue, integrating a set of local-to-local plants, which serve a specific market with a wide range of products and services, into a global operation that serves a wider market may be the best way to rationalize capacity. Multinational operations also have an issue of capacity rationalization. Instead of building a production facility in every country, the firm can build one large-scale production facility to take advantage of economies of scale in a location that serves a region of countries with similar tastes and relatively homogeneous markets.

Technology Transfer
1. Is the technology proprietary?
2. Is technology spillover a serious problem without appropriate patent protection?
3. Is technology transfer hard to implement?

When the technology is proprietary and the company is concerned about losing its technological edge, exporting operations may be less risky than the potential loss of the proprietary technology. When the technology can be easily imitated without patent protection, and it is undesirable for the company to be involved in direct investment in foreign countries, licensing may be a reasonable alternative. However, sometimes the technology transfer through licensing may prove to be difficult to implement. For instance, the transfer of intangible know-how has much to do with the sender's communication skill and the receiver's ability to understand. An ongoing relationship between the sender and the receiver may be required to make the transmission of knowledge work. The transfer of technology may take years or even have to operate on a continuing basis. In these cases, joint ventures may be more effective.

Availability of Materials and Components
1. Does availability of materials and components pose a constraint?
2. What is the cost of materials and components?

When production relies heavily on special types of natural resources, facilities obviously must be located with access to the resources. The cost and availability of materials should probably be considered of equal importance as a location factor as the nearness of markets.

Transportation
1. Does availability of transportation modes pose a problem?
2. What is the cost of transportation?
3. How reliable is the freight service?

In North America and Europe, the transportation infrastructure is well established. A well-connected web of routes served by airlines, trains, trucks, and ships can reach remote sites. However, in many developing countries, accessibility is still constrained by the lack of efficient transportation. When the product has a short shelf life and the only way to reach a local market is by land transportation, exporting operations may not be practical. When the transportation costs are so high that exporting a product is too expensive, localized and multinational operations should be considered. There exist many unforeseeable factors that could affect the reliability of international transportation. When the reliability of the freight service seriously affects a firm's production efficiency and competitiveness, it may want to structure global operation facilities with geographical proximity in mind.

Destination of global operations. Choosing a potential country for the site of globalizing operations is a tough decision since it involves many uncertainties and risks. Once a site has been chosen and the relevant investment sunk, it is very costly to reverse that decision. When something disastrous happens, such as an outbreak of war or regional instability, it may be too late for the company to pull out its investment. The decision of choosing a host country for globalizing operations can be based on an analysis of the host country's political stability, legal system, governmental policy, and infrastructure.

Political
1. Is the region politically stable?
2. Is the country politically stable?

There are three major types of political risks according to Czinkota, et al. (1992). In the first, the owners risk loss of property and life; in the second, the operating risk exposes the ongoing operations of a firm to outside interference; and in the third, transfer risk occurs when attempts are made to transfer funds between countries.

Legal System
1. Is the legal system complete?
2. Is the political system above the law?
3. Does the country comply with international laws?
4. Does the country have specific laws concerning foreign investment?

Foreign countries' legal systems provide another indicator of the local business environment. There are two major types of law: common law, which is based on tradition and follows precedent and custom, and code law, which depends on a comprehensive set of written statues. Legal systems can vary extensively in their philosophy, content, format, scope, and implementation. Some countries have a more comprehensive legal system, whereas others are more primitive in that respect. When the host country does not have a well-established legal system, foreign companies may find themselves in a disadvantageous position in case of conflicts between foreign and local companies. For example, a software company may find itself helpless in a country that neither complies with nor vigorously enforces internationally recognized patent and copyright laws. Countries whose government strongly encourages foreign investment have set more favorable procedures and rules with regard to foreign investment. Since these are usually administrative polices rather than laws, they are subject to changes.

Government Policy
1. Does the local government have specific sets of rules and procedures that impact foreign organizations?
2. Do environmental regulations, employment practices, and tax incentives favor foreign investment?

Host government's policies with respect to foreign investment have an important impact on the willingness of foreign investors to invest in that country and on the form of investment. The European Economic Community requires that foreign corporations doing business in the EEC must have at least 70 percent of the components manufactured locally for final assembly. Some developing nations insist that foreign companies export a certain fraction of the locally manufactured products and components to increase their foreign currency base. Trade conditions such as limitations on the flow of capital, people, and materials across borders, environmental regulations, employment practices, tax treaties between the host country and the domestic country, and tax incentives differ from one country to another. They have a significant impact on foreign investors' decision in choosing their investment destination and the form of investment.

Infrastructure
1. Are most areas of the country easily accessible?
2. What is the most common mode of transportation?
3. Is a distribution network well established?
4. Are communication systems efficient and connected to international routes?
5. Is availability of natural resources a constraint?
6. Does the country have the skilled labor that businesses require?
7. Does the country have well-trained management personnel?
8. What is the overall production cost?

One of the prerequisites for developing countries to achieve economic success is the development of a transportation infrastructure. Hong Kong and Singapore have a geographical advantage in that they are readily accessible by sea and by air, which partly explains the economic success of those regions. The distribution channels are also important.

Other Considerations
1. What is the official language in the host country?
2. Is the quality of life acceptable?
3. What are the locals' general attitudes towards foreign investment?

English is the most popular language in the world. It is also widely used in the business world. U.S. companies doing business in Britain, Australia, New Zealand, India, Canada, Singapore, Hong Kong, and Nigeria certainly experience much fewer communication problems since English is the (or at least one) official language in these countries. Quite a large population in the Netherlands, Belgium, Germany, Norway, Sweden, Switzerland, and Austria are bilingual. Flemish, Dutch, French, and German are the official languages in Belgium. Since the quality of life is generally better in developed countries than in developing countries, some expatriates are more willing to be assigned to developed countries. On the other hand, working in a developing country may appeal to someone who is averse to the high cost of living in cosmopolitan centers and is interested in seeking a unique cultural experience. People in some regions are considered more receptive to foreigners while people in other regions are considered more reserved. The local community's attitudes towards foreign investment is an important consideration in choosing the site because no business in a new environment can exist or prosper without the community's support.

Stage III. Operational Considerations

Once the company has decided the form and destination of global operations, it has to do more detailed planning. At this stage, the company has to consider issues such as operations strategy, location, productivity and quality, materials management, facility location and layout, technology management, and project management, which are the focuses of this book.

REFERENCES

Czinkota, M. R. P., P. Rivoli, and I. A. Ronkainen (1992). *International Business* (2nd ed.). Fort Worth: The Dryden Press.

Schroeder, R. (1993). *Operations Management: Decision Making in the Operations Function* (3rd ed.). New York: McGraw-Hill.

Sheth, J. and G. Eshghi (1992). *Global Operations Perspectives*. Cincinnati: South-Western Publishing.

Global Operations Strategy

Operations managers have four essential focuses, represented in Figure 3–1:

1. Quality. The products and services must meet or exceed the standards set by customers.
2. Productivity. The manager must find ways to improve productivity without sacrificing quality or morale.
3. Strategy. The global operations strategy must be consistent with the firm's industry strategy. It should be unique and a source of competitive advantage.
4. Serving the human trilogy: customers, employees, and shareholders.

The quality movement brought a new customer focus and awareness to business. Managers have two additional and equally important constituencies: employees, and shareholders. Deming (1982) insisted that a quality focus will lead to increased return on investment and profits.

Those managers who keep their eyes on the shareholder constituency at the expense of the other two groups will ultimately discover themselves with no one to manage and no group to cater to. It is a critical mistake to manage around the bottom line, maneuvering to manipulate short-term performance. If the first two components of this human trilogy, the customers and employees, are well served, the long-term success of the firm will reflect that fact.

An organization with a customer focus concentrates on exceeding the customer's expectations. These expectations must be well understood

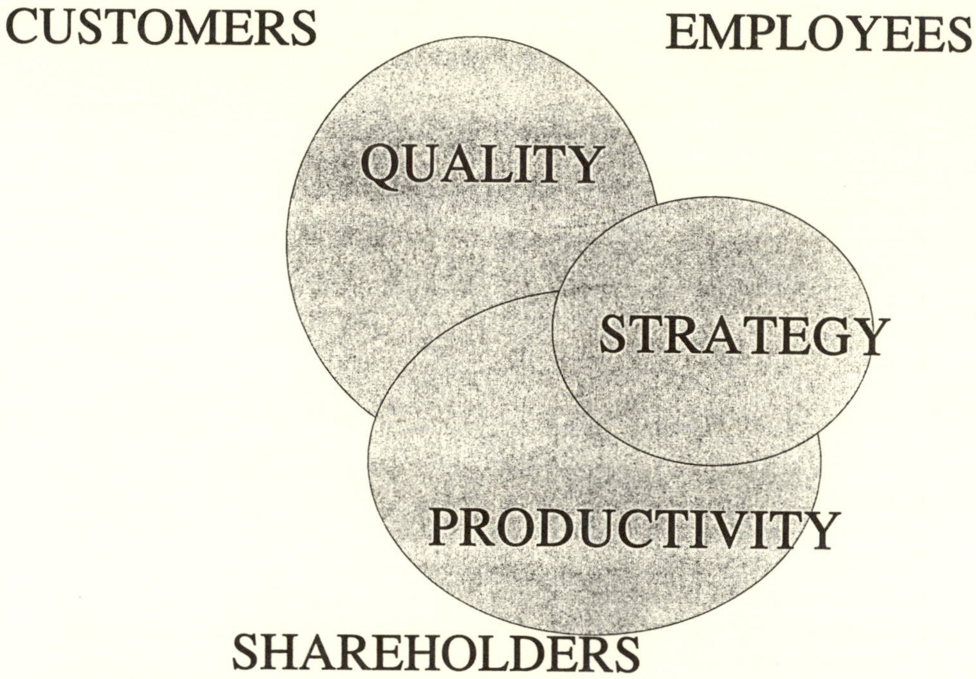

CUSTOMERS   EMPLOYEES

QUALITY

STRATEGY

PRODUCTIVITY

SHAREHOLDERS

Figure 3-1 Operations Management Focuses

by management and in line with company strategy. The product or service should do more for the customer than the customer has a right to expect.

A restaurant that advertises that it features an "all-you-can-eat food bar for only $3.99," will meet the customers' expectations if customers have to let their belts out a notch at the end of a meal. Customers may be somewhat pleased that they must rely on antacids the rest of the evening, for they have achieved what they intended—stuffing themselves silly for a low price. Another restaurant may charge its customers $50 for a meal. In this case, the customer expects the waiter or waitress to anticipate their wants and needs. Yet, if you were to stand outside both restaurants and ask customers, "On a scale of 1 to 5, 5 being best, how satisfied were you with your dining experience?" You might be surprised to discover that the all-you-can-eat place scored as high as the expensive restaurant. It is because the cheaper restaurant is able to meet customer expectations as well as the fancier establishment.

A customer focus has been well enunciated in the early 1990s. Companies should similarly strive to exceed the expectations of their employees. This can be accomplished through pay, promotions, benefits, or just plain surprises. "Because of your outstanding performance last month, every one will get an extra vacation day this year!" It may be difficult to imagine a company exceeding expectations during lean times, but allegiance to the employees during hard periods is critical to long-term success. Bonuses should never be awarded to senior managers who achieve cost savings by laying off workers. The size of the workforce often grows too large in the first place from years of poor planning, and managers should not reward themselves for later recognizing the error of their ways.

This chapter examines the global strategic management of operations. Operations was not viewed as a strategic area of the firm until the Japanese demonstrated to the world how truly strategic operations can be.

CATEGORIES OF OPERATIONS STRATEGY

Most of the literature on operations strategy has been aimed at manufacturing. In this chapter, manufacturing and service operations strategy are included under the broad heading, "operations strategy."

Operations strategies are functional strategies that support the firm's overall strategy. Porter (1985) argued that all corporations used some form of three basic strategies: low-cost production, differentiation, and cost or differentiation focus. Within the context of a firm's strategy, operations seeks to enhance the competitiveness of the business.

For years, the role of operations was simply to get the product or service out the door. The major voices in corporate strategy were in finance and marketing. However, the oil embargo of the mid-1970s helped change all that. Rising prices of gasoline sent customers all over the world in search of automobiles that optimized fuel consumption. The Japanese automobile manufacturers, especially Toyota and Nissan, had such vehicles available, and when customers flocked to try them, they noticed that the Japanese automobile was of superior quality. The Japanese had previously captured the electronics and camera markets through product quality, and suddenly, all Japanese products were purchased with customer confidence.

The first major writer in the U.S. to advocate the use of manufacturing as a competitive weapon was Wickham Skinner, a Harvard business professor. Skinner (1978) augured the dangers of forgetting the product and concentrating on financial strategies for growth. The early 1980s saw a series of articles published in the Harvard Business Review, including, "Managing Our Way to Economic Decline," authored by

Robert Hayes and William Abernathy (1980), which served as a call to action for American business. These authors made several points:

1. The Japanese were masters of using manufacturing as a competitive weapon.
2. American managers were sacrificing their long-term future for the short-term bottom line, delaying capital expenditures and plant improvements so that their personal performance evaluations would not be adversely effected by the outflow of expenses.
3. American corporations were trying to create the illusion of growth and dynamism through financial chicanery. Mergers, acquisitions, divestitures, leveraged buy-outs, and junk bonds were the toys of the arsenal, and the end result was that Americans were forgetting to improve their products. That was their ultimate failure in the global marketplace.

Hayes and Wheelwright's 1984 book *Restoring Our Competitive Edge* laid out the framework for manufacturing strategy, demonstrating a number of ways that manufacturing could be used to competitive advantage. *Restoring Our Competitive Edge* provided a catalogue of operations strategies, proving to be a very influential book for both practicing managers and academics. Hayes and Wheelwright listed eight major areas in which firms could seek competitive advantage in manufacturing: the workforce, vertical integration, facilities, capacity, quality, production planning and control, organization, and technology.

This book was followed by Hayes, Wheelwright and Clark's, *Dynamic Manufacturing* (1988). In the second book, the authors analyzed why some firms were excellent manufacturing firms and others were not. They found four themes predominating in the excellent manufacturing firms:

1. Management makes the difference.
2. The importance of a holistic perspective.
3. Relentlessly pursuing customer value.
4. Continuous learning.

In the 1990s, there appear to be ten major categories of operations strategies:

1. Designing for manufacturability
2. Flexible manufacturing
3. Speed to the marketplace
4. Quality and customer service
5. Technology management

6. Human resources in operations
7. Facilities location and layout strategies
8. Materials management
9. Organizational configuration and coordination
10. Sourcing

The strategic aspects of these ten categories are reviewed in this chapter. The more tactical aspects of these areas will be addressed in subsequent chapters.

Designing for Manufacturability

The most famous case of designing for manufacturability (DFM) was the development of the IBM Pro-printer. To develop their printer, IBM put together a team of product designers, manufacturing managers, and marketing managers. This team produced a printer that met and exceeded the customer's requirements and was easy to manufacture. At the other end of the spectrum was the development of the Gillette Sensor razor, a product that was developed without manufacturing input. The product proved very costly and difficult to manufacture. Luckily for Gillette, the product was welcomed in the marketplace.

DFM's purpose is not simply to make a product easier to produce. Obviously, an easy-to-manufacture product that nobody wants to buy is not worth much. New product development must be aimed at the ultimate customer, so it is imperative that DFM teams receive some form of customer input. Firms competing in global markets must consider the wants and needs of all customer groups, the manufacturing capabilities of their plants, and marketing across borders.

Flexible Manufacturing

It is infinitely easier to produce a limited product line at a plant than a broader line. Today's reality is that the product life cycle is shorter than ever and customers are fickle. This requires a manufacturing configuration that can adapt quickly to changing demand patterns. Machinery and equipment should be considered for purchase that can not only manufacture the current product but also be retooled for future changes in the product.

It is to operations' advantage to limit the number of options a customer can buy. Options mean more time. All customers do not have the same needs and wants, and companies that have the operational capability of offering customers *exactly* what they want, when they want it, have a competitive edge. Those that compete from a cost perspective may find it advantageous to limit options. The "focused" factory, one that specializes in a narrow product mix, thereby smoothing the production process by improving quality and productivity, makes sense for long product life cycles. The new factory must be both focused and flexible.

Flexibility is the key word at Toshiba. Toshiba President Fumio Sato led a campaign to " . . . make more products with the same equipment and people." Toshiba produces 20 varieties of laptop computers on the same assembly line and nine different word processors on another. Product life cycles are so short in the personal computer industry that such behavior is a competitive necessity (*Fortune*, September 21, 1992, pp. 61–74).

Toyota installed flexible lines and was able to cut setup times for new models in half through a technique they called "intelligent pallets"—computer-controlled pallets that make adjustments for different models.

Shortened product life cycles increase the need for simultaneous or concurrent engineering. Software designers have devised ways to facilitate the transfer of geometric data between CAD and CAM.

Speed to the Marketplace

At one time, it was true that firms could compete within an industry on the basis of offering superior quality to the customer. Mercedes-Benz in the automobile industry, Maytag in the appliance industry, and American Express in the financial services industry, all successfully used quality as a method of differentiating the products from competition. In the 1990s, the quality movements across the world succeeded in improving the quality of all products and services to the point that *all* companies must have superior quality merely to survive. As a result, the one way companies can gain an edge is to introduce new and innovative products *faster* than competition.

The product design cycle has been diminishing as a reaction to increased competition and quality and decreasing product life cycles. CAD-CAM have been instrumental tools in reducing this cycle.

New product introductions are a primary area where speed matters. Research and development, marketing, and operations must work together to determine which markets will be served and who will serve them. Product life cycles vary globally. It was once said that fashion took three or more years to reach Georgia from New York and California. This is no longer true, as a visit to any mall in Atlanta will attest. But this phenomenon still exists to some extent from one country to another and will influence the global staggering of new product introductions.

Speed continues to be the competitive issue in services. Credit card and travelers check companies pride themselves in speedy replacements of lost or stolen credit cards or travelers checks, no matter where in the world the customers are. Hotels have sped up the process of checking out, by allowing customers to check out through television sets. Hospitals have reduced the time to admit and discharge patients. A woman can deliver a baby and be back in her home in 24 to 36 hours. Rental cars are processed through hand-held processors that read a bar code from the automobile and immediately print the invoice.

Pizza is delivered to our homes, guaranteed (in urban areas) in 30 minutes. We can watch the news or weather reports whenever we want. We have become accustomed to the speed of a smaller world. This causes managers to work actively on the next generation of products before the previous generation has been announced to the public.

Quality and Customer Service

Most firms in capital intensive industries have implemented quality management programs by 1996. It is also true that the management commitment to quality varies.

Companies must produce to the needs of the most discriminating customer. Procter & Gamble's Pampers diapers are produced to satisfy the most quality-conscious costumer in the world, the Japanese. European buyers are demanding that products be certified with the European stamp of quality, ISO 9000.

A global customer-service network is imperative to maintain success. A product that has no locally-established service is asking for trouble when a problem occurs. It is not a simple question of choosing to sell a product in Thailand. A service network must also be established. The quality of customer service is as important as the actual quality of the product itself, because future customers can be gained or lost through customer service. American Express, Federal Express, United Parcel Service, Honda, and Mercedes are all known for their customer service networks across the world.

Technology Management

There are two aspects to the operations management of technology. The first aspect concerns process: every industry has a unique state-of-the-art process technology. For the manager, this involves a mastery of all possible process technologies that are either in use, or show potential for use, in the production of a product or service.

The second aspect concerns product technology. Firms must sell the technology that customers want. This means that managers must predict technological shifts. Companies don't want to be selling 286 computers when customers desire pentium computers.

Managers must stay current in new layouts and equipment that might increase productivity, quality, and profitability.

This necessitates a life-long commitment to the study of industry trade journals, scientific periodicals, general business publications, and any other sources that may offer technological information. The majority of managers have an inadequate scientific and mechanical educational background, which they must remedy if they intend to master their field.

Three ways managers can stay on top of technology are (1) attendance at trade shows and seminars, (2) trips to firms in other industries for benchmarking, and (3) frequent reading of a wide variety of industry-specific, general, and scientific journals.

Human Resources in Operations

How are human resources strategic? The answer is through the knowledge and skills of the work force. The most precious and un-inventoriable assets a company possesses are the knowledge and skills of its people. One company can outperform another company within the same industry simply because they work better and smarter, are more committed, and know more.

To achieve this state of employee performance requires an organizational climate in which people are recognized as the company's best asset and not just a bunch of replaceable heads. The top management team sets the tone for this climate.

One feature of a mobilized workforce is continuing education. Training budgets should be the last line to slash. Employees need to stay abreast of current trends through mechanisms such as trade shows, management seminars, management development courses, tuition reimbursement for college-level courses, and leaves of absences for educational redeployment.

The global organization brings the necessity of language skills and multicultural diversity. Many firms have established customer service and reservation centers in Salt Lake City, Utah, due to the availability of a multilingual workforce. This is peculiar to Utah because of the large number of returning Mormon missionaries from international missions.

A valuable global manager is one who has served terms in more than one country. The acronym IBM was once said to stand for "I've Been Moved," as the giant computer firm moved its managers all over the world. This strategy may be the predominate one for managers deemed to be the leaders of the future.

Facilities Location and Layout Strategies

In the 1970s and 1980s, manufacturers located plants in countries where labor was cheap. This phenomenon created a "hollow corporation," in which manufacturing was done in whatever foreign country featured the cheapest labor.

Cost cannot be the only consideration. Other important considerations include:

1. Maintaining a presence in an area of many customers.
2. Establishing a portfolio of plants to hedge against exchange rate fluctuations or political instability, enabling a speedy shift to production in the other plants.
3. The quality of the workforce and quality of the output. Poor quality can take away all the cost advantages of outsourcing to a low-cost plant.

Internal plant layout can be a source of efficiency or inefficiency. A well-designed layout can minimize cycle time and help get the product to the customer faster.

Materials Management

The Japanese proved to the world that the best solution to materials management was to design a "pull" system, one that produces to meet customer orders rather than to build inventory and minimizes inventory investment. In periods of high interest rates, it is extremely costly to pay for the luxury of buffer inventories.

Materials managers perform the balancing act of trying to provide materials while minimizing their materials investment. It is always an advantage to be able to promise product to a customer whenever the customer wants it. On the other hand, manufacturers realize an advantage if they don't begin to build product until they actually have an order. Here, effective inventory systems become critical.

In industries requiring assembly manufacturing, the mastery of the materials resource planning (MRP) software can give companies a significant planning capability that, if not duplicated by another firm in the industry, could provide a competitive advantage.

Organizational Configuration and Coordination

The organizational design of a firm, if effectively configured for decision-making, can give operations a decided edge in the marketplace. Organizations must limit their layers of management to remain agile.

Coordination among operations and the other functional areas, particularly research and development, marketing, and cost accounting, must be smooth. Geographical and cultural barriers complicate the flow of materials among plants, and a well-oiled distribution machine must be constructed from the functional parts of the firm, with the aim of serving customers effectively.

Sourcing

Procurement must take a stance on whether they intend to source materials from a selected few vendors or offer the business to many sources. The advantages of single sourcing include reduction in paperwork, fewer trucks to receive products from, the possibility of developing long-term relationships and partnerships, and lower prices. Multiple sourcing used to be the preferred approach in the United States, forcing vendors to bid for business annually. Business was often awarded on the basis of price alone. American buyers are now following the method of Japanese and Korean buyers in reducing their vendor relationships.

The move to single sourcing left many smaller firms at a disadvantage because they did not offer the "one stop shopping" available with larger competitors. These firms were forced to find niche markets in order to survive.

The sourcing question—whether to source from local, domestic, or foreign suppliers—should be a matter of price, quality, delivery dependability, and service.

STRATEGIC PRIORITIES FOR DIFFERENT NATIONS

We have previously discussed the various strategies that can be used in global operations. Some strategies are valued more highly by some companies than by others. Companies in one country may rank some strategies as more pertinent to them than companies in another country. A survey reported by Ferdows and his colleagues (1985) indicates companies in Europe, North America, and Japan have different competitive priorities. In 1984, the top competitive priorities for European firms were consistent quality, high performance products, dependable deliveries, low prices, and rapid design changes; for North American companies, they are consistent quality, high performance products, dependable deliveries, fast deliveries, and low prices; for Japanese firms, they are low prices, rapid design changes, consistent quality, high-performance products, and dependable deliveries. There appeared an agreement between top management in European and North American countries on focusing on quality as the top priority, while Japanese counterparts seemed to be more concerned with reducing production costs. This divergence may indicate that Japanese companies, having achieved higher levels of consistent quality, were seeking a new competitive weapon in low prices, whereas European and North American firms were still catching up with what they perceived to be lacking—quality. Another divergence is that North American and European firms tended to weigh more heavily the ability to produce high-performance product, whereas their Japanese counterpart put higher priority on the ability to respond to rapid design changes.

United States

Quality has been the driving force for U.S. companies since the 1980s. Based on the Global Manufacturing Roundtable survey (Miller et al., 1992), manufacturing action plans have changed from production inventory systems, reduction in workforce, supervisor training, direct labor motivation, and process/product development in 1984 to vendor quality, statistical quality control, worker safety, manufacturing strategy, and worker training in 1988. U.S. firms perceived their relative competitive strengths in 1990 as reliable products, high-performance product design, and low defect rates; at the same time, they perceived their weaknesses as the inability to develop and design new products quickly and to compete on prices. The top action plan for 1990 is to link manufacturing and business strategy.

European Countries

The unification of European markets creates a favorable business environment for most European manufacturers. The same survey (Miller et al., 1992) indicates that the top competitive priorities for European manufacturers as a group in 1990 are offering consistently low defect rates, offering dependable delivery, and providing reliable/durable products. When asked about their future direction, two thirds of the respondents said they intended to build a market share in the period from 1990 to 1995, a clear change of focus from stressing quality to building market share.

Japan

Japan has certainly built a strong case for product quality. From 1988 to 1990, they reported improvements in inventory reduction, the number of products produced in a plant, and setup time reduction and continued quality improvement (Miller et al., 1992). Their top action plans were largely responsible for these improvements. In 1988, they ranked reducing manufacturing lead time, improving production control systems, reducing procurement lead time, improving time for design change, and increasing ability to introduce new product as their top action plans. Their top manufacturing objectives in 1990 were reducing unit cost, improving conformance quality, and improving direct labor productivity, which aimed at reducing cost to increase market share.

A STUDY OF TWO INDUSTRIES*

Machine Tools

Environmental conditions within an industry constrain the tactics and strategies employed by operations managers. A recent study of operations strategies employed in the machine tools and textile industries illustrated the impact of environmental conditions on manufacturing. The objective of the study was to compare international production practices within the context of industry capabilities and manufacturing strategy.

An international research team, including researchers from the Korea Productivity Center, the Sogang Institute for Economics and Business, the Shanghai Institute of Mechanical Engineering, IMD (the international business school in Lausanne, Switzerland), and the Business School at Indiana University collected data in China, Korea, Japan, Western Europe, and the United States (Rho and Whybark, 1988).

There were tremendous differences among the countries' capabilities in the machine tools industry. China's machine tools were described as of inferior quality and technologically primitive. The tools were not carefully engineered and less durable than those produced in other nations. The machine tool industry primarily provided tools to the Chinese defense industry. Little export of Chinese machine tools takes place. The industry was updating technologically and importing advanced technology tools, primarily from Japan, the United States, Switzerland, and West Germany (Davenport, 1988).

In 1975, Japan ranked fourth in the world and produced half as many machine tools as the U.S. By 1982, Japan had captured the world lead and in 1990 possessed over half of the market share in the United States.

*Portions of this section previously appeared in Young, S. T., K. Kwong, C. Li, and W. Fok, "Manufacturing Strategies and Practices: A Study of Two Industries," *International Journal of Operations and Production Management*, 12(9):5–17, 1992.

Import quotas were finally instituted to stem the tide of Japanese machine tools into the U.S. The Japanese took the world lead by introducing less expensive and easier-to-operate, numerically controlled (NC) machine tools. By being at the leading technology edge, Japan quickly gained the world lead in the industry trends of automated and unmanned systems using new materials (Sarathy, 1989).

In 1987, West Germany manufactured 62 percent, Italy 18.6 percent, the United Kingdom 9.3 percent, and France 8.7 percent of the machine tools in Western Europe (Business Japan, 1987). In the period from 1978 to 1984, West Germany, Italy, the United Kingdom, and France suffered an average of 28 percent reduction in the industry workforce, with the U.K. seeing a 59 percent reduction in the size of its workforce. These hits were caused by lost business to Far Eastern suppliers and an overall industry recession in the early 1980s. In terms of sales, the U.K. dropped 27 percent in this seven year period, while West Germany, France, and Italy slightly increased sales. Also, there were 10 percent fewer factories in Western Europe in 1984 than in 1975.

With the Western European aims of reducing manufacturing costs, achieving more flexibility, and shortening processing times (Business Japan, 1987), there was an expected increase in the use of CAD-CAM, numerically controlled machine tools, FMS (Flexible manufacturing systems), and cellular manufacturing. Within Western Europe, the ability of many of the U.K. firms to meet these challenges was perhaps the most serious concern.

The U.S. machine tools industry, the world leader from World War II to the early 1980s, held a global share of less than 10 percent by 1989 (Holland, 1989). One cause of this decline was the cheap licensing of technology to Japanese machine tool makers in exchange for Far Eastern marketing channels. Numerically controlled machine tools were invented in the United States, but it was the Japanese manufacturers who became the standard bearers for the technology. The U.S. industry rebounded somewhat from a perilous low in 1982, but a trade agreement was necessary to limit Japanese imports. Japanese firms have since circumvented the agreements by locating plants in the United States and 30 percent of the U.S. machine tool capacity was Japanese owned by 1990 (Standard and Poors Industry Surveys, 1990).

Textiles

China is the world's largest textile producer, and textiles are its greatest export. China competes against Korea in the lower-quality end of the textiles market and has lower labor costs than Korea. China was 15th in the world in textiles in 1973 and sixth by 1983 (The World Bank, 1987).

Textiles are also Korea's greatest export. Sixty-two percent of the textiles produced in Korea are exported. However, structural changes jeopardized Korea's global strength. There have been significant technical innovations in the arts of spinning and weaving, while Korea is burdened with older machines. Rising domestic wage rates have also hurt Korea's textile industry. The average Korean works 2,833 hours a year compared with 2,168 for the Japanese (Kang, 1989). Quality improvements in the industry have been slow and productivity has diminished.

Korea, Hong Kong, Taiwan, and China threatened Japan's textile industry to the extent that they took a third of the Japanese market. Japan lost share primarily in the lower-cost and lower-quality markets and countered by moving to the production of materials requiring technological capabilities beyond the reach of Asian competitors. Innovative machinery and large investments in research and development are characteristics of the Japanese textile industry.

Germany adopted a textile industry strategy similar to that of Japan. The Germans turned from competition with the low-cost Far Eastern countries to production of specialty products (Commission of the European Communities, 1986). The German industry can be described as highly specialized with high productivity. The German banking industry was very involved in the decisions of German textile manufacturing because they had a high equity stake in the industry. Government assistance was minimal.

Among other European countries, only Italy increased its global market share in recent years. Italy succeeded due to factors such as geographical production concentrations that reduced transportation costs, lower labor costs from locations in high unemployment areas, and the use of modern technology and modern management practices, including computerized inventory control. The U.K. textile industry has declined since 1973, a victim of recession, Far Eastern competition, and failed strategies. The U.K. productivity in the textile industry was approximately half that of the U.S. textile industry (Ghadar, Davidson and Feigenoff, 1987).

Imports seriously affected labor-intensive and short-run fabric markets in the U.S. textiles industry (Standard and Poors Industry Surveys, 1990). In reaction, U.S. manufacturers de-emphasized products that couldn't compete with the imports and focused their efforts on domestics, including sheets, towels, and pillowcases. In 1990, domestic mills operated at capacity, primarily supplying domestic markets. The trade deficit in textiles was enormous. In 1977, 743 million pounds of textiles were exported and 1,286 million pounds were imported. Ten years later, 913 million pounds were exported and 4,417 million pounds were imported.

Manufacturing Strategy

Several manufacturing strategy areas outlined by Hayes and Wheelwright (1984) are pertinent in these industries: quality, production planning, technology, and the work force.

Japanese quality control was world renowned, with empirical and anecdotal evidence supporting its superiority (Schonberger, 1982; Garvin, 1986). Korean quality, while not taken as seriously as the Japanese, appears to meet competitive standards. Japan was the world leader in machine tools, with quality and technology being the driving reasons. China has struggled to provide adequate tools for its own domestic needs due to its inferior quality, production planning and technology.

The Chinese workforce expected lifetime employment in the past, but in 1986, domestic labor reforms instituted labor contracts in which either the employer or employee could decide not to renew at the expiration of the contract (Horsley, 1988). The typical Chinese worker took home $45 a month, including a $10 bonus. Chinese managers appealed to the workers' moral and political motivations rather than material motivations. The state establishes production quotas and profits are appropriated by the government and allocated for units that experience losses. As a result, state enterprises have little motivation to exceed their quotas (Zhuang and Whitehill, 1989).

Before World War II, Great Britain's spinning and weaving technologies were the world standard. Since that time, U.S.-based technologies dominated the industry, and by the 1980s the U.S. was generally regarded as having the most productive and cost-efficient industry in the world (Toyne et al., 1984). The Far East became strong because much of the textile industry was labor-intensive. West Germany succeeded with a strategy of offshore manufacturing to take advantage of the labor cost differential (labor in Germany is more expensive than in the United States). Great Britain has not used this strategy as a matter of principle, and the U.S. was prohibited from this practice by Item 807 of the Tariff Schedule of the United States, which does not prohibit offshore manufacturing for the apparel industry.

The machine tools industry is one in which the Japanese are in the forefront of technology and innovation, with firms in other countries following their lead. In Europe, there were decided differences in the strategic use of the work force between Great Britain and Germany. Germany employed a formal system of vocational training that led to a lifetime career. Vocational training was followed by a two-or three-year apprenticeship. Such a system contributed to an international reputation for skill in manufacturing. Great Britain's weaknesses in manufacturing were partly attributed to their poor development of human resources (Commission of the European Communities, 1986). Training was carried out within the plant, so the British plant learning curve could be expected to be longer than that of a German plant.

Government involvement in industry strategies was extensive. Most governments were protectionist for both industries and involved in recommending global industry strategies. South Korea actually prohibited textile imports unless they were re-exported. The United States limited Japanese imports in the machine tools industry. Only Germany could be described as laissez-faire, welcoming a free market.

Firms within these industries varied their strategies, but industry strategies could be classified into a global competitive scheme, based on their industry competitive orientation. Porter (1990) recommended sharply limiting direct cooperation among industry rivals, arguing Western governments have misunderstood the role of the Japanese Ministry of International Trade and Industry (MITI). MITI projects work best in stimulating proprietary research and Japanese firms do not contribute their best engineers and scientists to cooperative projects.

Hayes and Wheelwright (1984) wrote that firms could be classified into four stages of manufacturing strategy:

Stage 1: Internally neutral. Production simply makes the product and ships it.

Stage 2: Externally neutral. Manufacturing merely meets the standards set by competition.

Stage 3: Internally supportive. Manufacturing attempts to become unique from its competition.

Stage 4: Externally supportive. Manufacturing pursues uniqueness on a global scale, becoming a world-class competitor.

According to the Hayes and Wheelwright framework, both Japanese industries could be considered stage 4 and the Korean industries stage 3. The Chinese textile industry was stage 3, but the Chinese machine tool industry stage 1. National industrial capability greatly constrains manufacturing in China as it enhances manufacturing in Japan.

Due to the divergence of European strategies, it was not possible to determine a unified strategy. The United States textile industry, with its heavy domestic market concentration, could be classified as stage 3 and the machine tools industry, so late to react to global trends, fits into stage 2.

The principles of quality and technological innovation that brought the Japanese success in the automobile and electronics industries could be found in the machine tools and textile industries. The survey did not reveal any strategic use of production planning practices other than the fact that the Japanese were faster at producing machine tools than the

Chinese, Europeans, and Americans. However, a competitive advantage was gained by simply outperforming the rest of the industry in production planning.

Korea has increasingly become an exporter to be reckoned with. The Japanese success formulas have been well documented and the Koreans seem to be following a similar pattern. The large-scale entrance of the People's Republic of China into international trade, clouded by the political events of 1989, was years away in the industries we analyzed. Presently, national policies and strategies and firm performances differ substantially among European countries in these industries and it is difficult to speculate on the global impact.

The relative absence of information systems for production planning in any of these countries could produce a source of competitive advantage for the United States. U.S. manufacturers have more information available for production planning than their Far Eastern competitors.

This research described global manufacturing practices and strategies in the machine tools and textiles. A lesson to be learned from this research is that studying international operations at the industry level is an approach that will yield information quite different from what is expected.

CONCLUSIONS

The environmental circumstances surrounding the machine tools and textiles industries are illustrative of the world surrounding the operations manager. Management takes place given a set of structural constraints that may change at a glacial pace or at the speed of light. To meet the company's objectives, operations managers must clearly understand the mission, direction, and purpose of the organization. With this understanding, it is then a challenging matter of arranging the management systems so that the workers can thrive and help achieve those objectives.

REFERENCES

"Brace for Japan's Hot New Strategy." *Fortune*, September 21, 1992, pp. 61–74.
Commission of the European Communities. (1986). *The Social Aspects of Technological Developments Relating to the European Machine-tool Industry*. Luxembourg: Office for Official Publications of the European Communities.
Davenport, A. (1988). "Forging a Modern Machine Tool Industry." *The China Business Review*, May-June: 38–44.
Deming, W. E. (1982). *Out of the Crisis*. Cambridge, MA: MIT Press.

Ferdows, K., J. G. Miller, J. Nakane, and T. E. Vollmann (1985). "Evolving global manufacturing strategies: Projections into the 1990s." *International Journal of Operations and Production Management*, 6(4):5–14.

Garvin, D. A. (1986). "Quality Problems, Policies, and Attitudes in the United States and Japan: an Exploratory Study." *Academy of Management Journal*, 29:653–673.

Ghadar, F., W. Davidson, and C. Feigenoff (1987). *U.S. Industrial Competitiveness*. Lexington, MA: Lexington Books.

Hayes, R. H. and W. J. Abernathy (1980). "Managing Our Way to Economic Decline." *Harvard Business Review*, July-August: 67–77.

Hayes, R. H. and S. C. Wheelwright (1984). *Restoring our Competitive Edge*. New York: John Wiley & Sons.

Hayes, R. H., S. Wheelwright, and K. B. Clark (1988). *Dynamic Manufacturing*. New York: The Free Press.

"Holding the Lead in the Machine Tool Industry Proves Tough." *Business Japan*, September, 1987, pp. 95–104.

Holland, M. (1989). *When the Machine Stopped*. Boston: Harvard Business School Press.

Horsley, J. P. (1988). "The Chinese Workforce." *The China Business Review*, May–June: 50–55.

Kang, T. W. (1989). *Is Korea the Next Japan?* New York: The Free Press.

Miller, J. G., A. De Meyer, and J. Nakane (1992). *Benchmarking Global Manufacturing*. Homewood, IL: Business One Irwin.

Porter, M. E. (1990). *The Competitive Advantage of Nations*. New York: The Free Press.

Porter, M. E. (1985). *Competitive Advantage*. New York: The Free Press.

Rho, B. and D. C. Whybark (1988). "Comparing Manufacturing Practices in the People's Republic of China and South Korea." *Working Paper No. 4*. Indiana University: Indiana Center for Global Business.

Sarathy, R. (1989). "The Interplay of Industrial Policy and International Strategy: Japan's Machine Tool Industry." *California Management Review*, 31(3):132–160.

Schonberger, R.J. (1982). *Japanese Manufacturing Techniques*. New York: The Free Press.

Skinner, W. (1978). *Manufacturing in the Corporate Strategy*. New York: John Wiley & Sons.

Standard & Poors Industry Surveys. (1990). New York: Standard & Poors.

Toyne, B., J. Arpan, A. Barnett et al. (1984). *The Global Textile Industry*. London: George Allen & Unwin.

The World Bank. (1987). *Korea: Managing the Industrial Transition*. Washington, DC: The World Bank.

Zhuang, S. C. and A. M. Whitehill (1989). "Will China Adopt Western Management Practices?" *Business Horizons*, March-April: 58–64.

4

Managing Productivity and Quality

MEASUREMENT SYSTEMS

This chapter addresses the management of productivity and quality, which is essentially what operations management is all about. Many of the tools and principles discussed here will be old news to experienced managers, since they have been using these tools for years. The emphasis here is on the management of these tools.

The total quality management (TQM) movement brought with it a need for a measurement system. Uniformity is key to any global organization's measurement approach. Senior operations managers must coordinate quality and productivity measurement systems so that they offer valid comparisons from plant to plant.

The measurement system should include a number of appropriate measurements, all focused on the quality of the product or service, and the input of the work force in accomplishing total output.

The most important consideration for global operations is that measurement systems are coordinated among plants. A Pareto analysis performed in a plant in France is valuable information to a sister plant in Italy. Information, measurement approaches, and TQM training should be implemented programmatically into all plants.

Garvin (1992) wrote about eight dimensions to quality:

1. Conformance: the ability of a product to meet customer specifications. An established manufacturing standard might be that a ball bearing is to be produced within a certain range of acceptable diameters. The ability to meet the specifications is conformance.

2. Aesthetics: the physical appearance of the product or the physical surroundings and ambience of the service. Several automobiles are so well designed that heads turn to watch these cars drive past. A few that come to mind in 1996 are the Mazda RX7, the Lexus 400, the Lincoln Mark VIII, and the Dodge Viper. Similarly, everyday products may appeal to the customer because of a radical innovation in design. The Apple Macintosh computer and the AT&T Slimline telephone were major design innovations. Good restaurants appreciate the effect ambience can have on a successful customer service encounter.

3. Perceived quality: the most important measurement of quality is what the customer *thinks* of product or service quality. Here, measurements of conformance, reliability, and performance are supplemental to the total effect of quality on the customer. It may indeed be that one manufacturer's toaster-oven has fewer defects than another manufacturer's, but if a survey of customer reveals that they perceive the inferior manufacturer to outperform the one with the best quality record, that is most important to ultimate sales. Of course, inferior quality will catch up with any manufacturer.

4. Reliability: the ability to meet expected performance time after time. If a car is supposed to be able to go from 0 to 60 mph in 6.3 seconds, it should do so 100 out of 100 times. If Federal Express promises next day delivery, 99 percent of the time, they should be able to maintain that reliability standard.

5. Durability: the product's ability to withstand stress and to last. Many products are not known for their product design, but for their sturdiness. Samsonite luggage used to feature a commercial in which a gorilla hurled Samsonite luggage all across his cage, jumping up and down on it, flinging it to and fro. This was exactly what airline passengers envisioned happening to their luggage once the conveyor belt passed it out of sight, so the commercial succeeded. Volvo and Mercedes stressed durability by showing auto crash tests. Brooks Brothers and Hart, Schaffner, and Marx are clothing manufacturers that feature timeless design and well-tailored suits that customers know are made to last.

6. Performance: the product's ability to do whatever the customer requires. An automobile's performance is measured by its time to reach 60 miles an hour, braking ability, and fuel consumption. A stereo is measured by its power output, signal-to-noise ratio, and frequency response. A package delivery service is measured by its delivery time.

7. Features: the "bells and whistles," items attached to the product that may increase the product's desirability. These may be standard items with the product or additional options, but the customer perceives that the value of the product increases with added features. All other things being equal, an automobile offering power windows and

locks is perceived to be of superior quality to one with manual windows.

8. Serviceability: the ability to repair a product, correct a service situation, or, in general, receive needed customer service. Customer service is perhaps equal in product quality in the customer's mind. If a customer has some problem, superior service can go a long way toward increasing customer loyalty. Any new product must include a service network in product release plans.

TOTAL QUALITY MANAGEMENT

Arnold Feigenbaum is generally credited with coining the phrase "total quality control," a phrase that evolved into "total quality management." TQM programs require a data-driven approach to management. A core principal of quality management is that you should be able to measure quality, and that involves a variety of tools. These include control charts, fishbone diagrams, Pareto diagrams, run charts, scatter diagrams, and frequency histograms.

Top-quality products and services are now a basic requirement for global survival. It is quite difficult to compete on the basis of quality when quality is almost a given in most industries. One company that learned quality lessons well is Federal Express. In the 1980s, Federal Express was dropped by Amsco as their courier of choice, primarily due to quality and service failures (Bowman, 1993). Federal Express identified their most frequent causes of service failures and embarked on a program of continuous improvement. After a comprehensive TQM campaign, Federal Express was able to recapture Amsco's business. Federal Express now follows up with quarterly service meetings with Amsco.

TQM was the most important managerial concept of the late 1980s and early 1990s. The key to the global success of TQM programs is consistency of implementation, measurement, and the willingness to share information across boundaries.

ISO 9000

In Europe, the quality requirements established by the International Organization for Standardization (ISO 9000) are quickly becoming the benchmark against which all companies are measured. This certificate, which shows customers how a company tests products, trains employees, keeps records, and fixes defects, is an accepted seal of quality approval, one no company marketing products in Europe can afford not to have.

Some product categories are considered "regulated" by the European Community (Belgium, Denmark, France, Germany, Greece, Ireland, Italy, Luxembourg, the Netherlands, Portugal, Spain, and the United Kingdom) and must be certified in ISO 9000.

The ISO 9000 series consists of five categories (Bureau of Business Practice, 1992):

1. ISO 9000. *Quality Management and Quality Assurance Standards— Guidelines for Selection and Use.*
2. ISO 9001. *Quality Systems—Model for Quality Assurance in Design/Development, Production, Installation, and Servicing.*
3. ISO 9002. *Quality Systems—Model for Quality Assurance in Final Inspection.*
4. ISO 9003. *Quality Systems—Model for Quality Assurance in Final Inspection and test.*
5. ISO 9004. *Quality Management and Quality System Elements—Guidelines.*

ISO certification is granted by a number of approved registrars. In the United States, an affiliate of the American Society for Quality Control (ASQC), the Registrar Accreditation Board (RAB) accredits registrars. AT&T, for example, has its own quality registrar. In 1991, AT&T's registrar spent 500,000 hours conducting quality audits of AT&T's suppliers (Bureau of Business Practice, 1992). AT&T's registration process consists of nine steps:

1. The application form.
2. The quality manual desk audit.
3. Preliminary evaluation.
4. The full audit.
5. Auditor's final report to Registration Board.
6. The appeals process.
7. Registration Board's decision.
8. Semiannual follow-up audits.
9. Triennial full audits.

Dupont drew a nine-step road map to ISO 9000 registration (see Figure 4–1. This road map delineates the extensive planning and organization that a registration effort requires. The process of improving quality in conjunction with Dupont's efforts for certification resulted in tremendous performance benefits (Bureau of Business Practice, 1992): cost reductions of $3 million at an electronics site and millions more in savings at other plants, on-time delivery improved from 70 to 90 percent, and cycle time of one product line reduced from 15 days to 1.5 days.

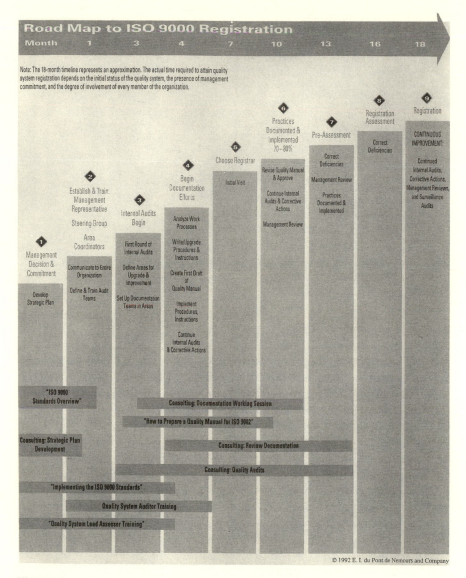

Figure 4-1

THE MALCOLM BALDRIGE AWARD CRITERIA (U.S.A.)

As part of a campaign to encourage the improvement of American products, the United States government began sponsorship of the Malcolm Baldrige National Quality Award in 1987. Patterned after the

Deming Prize, the highest award for quality in Japan, this award is presented annually to deserving manufacturers, service companies, and small businesses.

Companies that apply for this award must undergo several stages of examination. A company is scored on their performance in seven categories:

1. Leadership (10 percent)
2. Information and analysis (7 percent)
3. Strategic quality planning (8 percent)
4. Human resource utilization (15 percent)
5. Quality assurance of products and services (14 percent)
6. Quality results (18 percent)
7. Customer satisfaction (30 percent)

This scoring system reveals the opinions of quality experts, however the most important criteria is how customers perceive quality.

PRODUCTIVITY MEASUREMENT

Companion to quality measurements are productivity measurements. Quality measurements tell the manager how well we are doing, and productivity measurements tell the manager the cost of doing it. Productivity is measured with some ratio of output to inputs such as labor dollars or labor hours.

The Japanese Productivity Center compared productivity in a number of countries with Japanese productivity. Table 4–1 provides a basis for comparison among several countries in key industries.

Some data from the U.S. automobile industry in the mid-1980s illustrates much about the difficulty in interpreting productivity measurements.

Honda		Jeep
850	autos/day	750
2432	workers	5000
1.7	plant size	5.0
	(million sq. ft.)	

Both plants were in the state of Ohio, with Honda in Marysville and Jeep in Toledo. A number of factors explain why the Jeep plant was less productive than the Honda plant: the Jeep plant produced more models—four wheel drives, two wheel drives, station wagons, etc., whereas the Honda plant produced one model. The Jeep plant had serious

Table 4–1
Global Industrial Productivity
(Index, Japan=1000)

Industry	Japan	U.S.	W. Germany	France	U.K.
Agriculture, forestry & fishing	100.0	338.4	163.4	223.0	254.8
Mining	100.0	204.8	34.7	66.2	*
Manufacturing	100.0	124.2	84.6	94.9	123.6
Electric, gas & water	100.0	59.0	59.1	59.3	86.5
Wholesale/retail trade	100.0	179.9	120.7	166.7	113.7
Finance/Insurance Real estate & business services	100.0	95.4	85.6	118.9	112.5

*Mining figure is included in Manufacturing in U.K.

(Source: *Worldwide Comparison of Labor Productivity.* Tokyo: Japan Productivity Center, Productivity Laboratory, 1991, pp.108–117)

discord between management and labor. The assembly line had been sabotaged, resulting in downtime that cost Jeep over a million dollars. The Honda plant had the advantage of being a newer plant, more efficiently designed, with more automation.

There are several other reasons why the Honda plant was more productive at that time, but the point is that there existed major differences in productivity within the same industry and same state. This illustrates that management and management systems have a great deal to do with productivity.

INDUSTRY MEASUREMENTS

All industries have productivity indicators that are important to managers. Here are some examples:

Health Care	Airlines	Credit Cards
Days per pt. stay	On-time arrival rate	Response to lost cards
Mortality	On-time departure rate	Charges/employee hr.
Avg. census/labor $	Baggage lost/labor hr.	Incorrect charges/hr.
Total costs/labor $	Passenger miles/labor $	New cards issued/hr.

All of these measurements should attempt to relate an important performance output to a form of input, such as labor dollars or hours.

Table 4–2

MCP/PMT

Hospital Performance

Criteria Score	Length of pt. stay (Avg. Days)	Census/labor hr. (Per Day)	Profit $/Month
10	3.5 Days	10	$500,000
9	3.7	11	475,000
8	3.9	12	450,000
7	4.1	13	425,000
6	4.3	14	400,000
5	4.5	15	375,000
4	4.7	16	350,000
3	4.9	17	325,000
2	5.1	18	300,000
1	5.3	19	275,000
Weight	.25	.25	.50

In the airlines industry, for example, the actual number of lost bags tell you less than the ratio of lost bags to employee hours. An airline downsizing its baggage department might expect to see an increase in lost bags. The measurement it would really want to watch would be the ratio of lost bags to employee hours. If it felt the downsizing was warranted, this ratio should diminish after a force reduction.

A manager may desire to aggregate a group of measurements into one overall productivity score. There are several approaches to multiple productivity scores. A form of linear programming, *data envelope analysis*, is one approach. This method compares the inputs and outputs of each measurement and selects the most efficient units relative to the other units. For further information on this technique, see Charnes, Cooper and Rhodes (1981); Sherman (1984); and Young (1989).

Perhaps a simpler method was suggested by D. Scott Sink (1985), the Multi Criterion Performance Measurement Technique (MCP/PMT) indexing method. This method begins with the selection of measurement criteria. For example, a hospital administrator might take the length of patient stay, patient census per labor hour, and profitability as three important measurements to aggregate. The next step is to determine a performance scale, with 10 points awarded to the best possible performance for each criteria. This scales down to a score of 1. Finally, a weighting is determined according to the relative importance of each criteria. The administrator may determine that profitability should include 50 percent of the total score, and the other two measures 25 percent each. The actual scores are compared with the scale and weights, providing an overall score. This score is used as an index from one period to the next.

These numbers may be way off base from the reality at other hospitals, but have meaning for this administrator. If, in one month, the average length of stay is 4.9 days, the census/labor hour rate is 16, and the profit is 375,000, the scores for the individual criterion would be 3 for length of stay, 4 for the census ration, and 5 for profitability. These scores multiplied by the weights yield $(3 \times 0.25) + (4 \times 0.25) + (5 \times 0.5)$ = 4.25. This score is then compared with scores from other months to give a picture of overall performance.

Some productivity measurements make no real contribution to the mission of the organization. The purpose of individual measurements should be addressed. Why do we want to know this? A jewelry department within a major department store in Atlanta measured the productivity of its clerks with the simple formula (sales, returns). The problem with the measurement was that the returns were counted against the person handling the return, not the clerk making the original sale. The result? Anytime a clerk saw a customer approaching the counter, carrying a bag that represented a potential return, the clerk would be reluctant to serve the customer. Here was a measurement that was actually causing negative behavior. The problematical system was finally pointed out to management and corrected with a simple program addition to the computer software.

Many productivity measurements should be questioned. These points should be considered:

1. No worker or manager's performance can be captured by one productivity measurement.
2. It pays to ask the workers about the validity of the current measurements and ask for suggestions on ways to more appropriately capture their performance.

Some workers, particularly white-collar employees, may resist measurement, but observation of their work should yield a method to quantify their output. For example, a private investigator might argue that his or her work is too difficult to quantify. The mission of the investigator leads to one important measurement: cases solved per labor hour.

Comparisons of plant productivity must consider differences in product mix, exchange rates, production systems, and labor rates before a valid analysis can be undertaken. A simple comparison of revenue per labor hour does not sufficiently capture plant productivity, and management must have an intuitive grasp of differences among a number of plants. It is a key principle that decision-making not be dictated by productivity measurements. The measurements provide fuel for analysis before decisions are made. It is helpful, however, that plants and offices within the same firm share productivity and quality measurements and benchmark successful programs.

MANAGING BLUE-COLLAR PRODUCTIVITY

The same management approaches do not work for blue collar, white-collar, and professional workers. Managers must discover their own methods to motivate each group to greater productivity. As we shall discuss in the chapter, "Human-Centered Production," a beginning point for managing any type of worker is to manage at their level, and this means understanding what makes them tick.

W. Edwards Deming believed that the desire to do good work was a human trait. What does an operations manager do when confronted with an atmosphere of distrust for management and a minimal interest in getting the work done well? These are the key questions to successful operations management, more essential than the correct matching of production schedules to labor schedules. The manager who can find the answer to these questions will find the going at work a lot more rewarding.

MANAGING WHITE-COLLAR PRODUCTIVITY

White-collar workers, on the average, have more education and make a greater income than blue-collar workers. Their productivity is more difficult to measure due to the intangibility of many forms of office work. The demographic trends of the 21st century point to a period in which college-educated individuals will experience a logjam in middle management and promotions will prove difficult. For those who seek responsibility, smaller organizations and entrepreneurial opportunities present the most hope. Meanwhile, back at the office, finding ways other than money to motivate these well-educated employees becomes a challenge.

Marlowe McGraw, an engineer in New Orleans, Louisiana, expressed a quite cynical view of the corporate world:

> I think it's sad that we are not able to allow people their own greatness within the corporate structure. People get squashed. There's got to be alternatives that would allow people to excel, to move to the areas they are best suited for. I look at the photographs of the people who are running a lot of the major organizations in this country, and I say you can learn a lot

from photographs. It wears on their faces, much of what they're about, and I don't aspire to that. The current president of our company gives quarterly updates on the state of the corporation. He speaks and looks as if he's a mortician. There's something about the rites of ascension that seem to beat too much out of individuals.

Abraham Lincoln said goodbye to someone, and then turned to his secretary and said, "I don't like his face."

She said, "That's a harsh way to judge someone."

He responded, "After 40 years of age, every one is responsible for his face."

That's what I'm talking about when I look at these photographs. I don't see the same kind of vision in their eyes or creases in their face that I see on the faces of poets, artists, musicians. Great scientists have it. The corporate world has somehow lost the ability to bring out the best in people. They might have 10 percent of the people operating at 75 percent of what they're capable of as a human being. Of the other 90 percent, they're "living lives of quiet desperation."

The intangibility of measuring performance output is one of the difficult aspects of white-collar production. A measurement system must be devised in which workers understand when they have achieved good output. Because their work is less machine-paced than a factory worker's, many office workers take time to socialize and talk with their fellow employees and lose focus on their work mission. Socialization is very important to performance, obviously, but over-socialization becomes problematic.

Managers in a foreign culture must understand the cultural norms of the office, focusing on desired performance without violating the right mix of work and play. Many office behaviors in one culture are unacceptable in others, and foreign managers must be well versed on what to expect before they embark on foreign assignments.

MANAGING PROFESSIONAL PRODUCTIVITY

Operations managers who lead a group of professionals, whether they are surgeons, professors, engineers, laboratory researchers, or psychologists, have a unique managerial challenge. Professionals value independence. Since no manager is any smarter than they are, they often will second-guess the manager. Perhaps the single most important aim of the operations manager of professionals is to get them to buy into a common mission. Give them freedom, give them the goal, let them decide how they will reach the goal, and let them go (within some boundaries, of course.) Managers of groups of professionals must make sure that the overachievers of the professional workforce work in concert with those less willing to make personal sacrifices. Some team chemistry is threatened when one member goes beyond the boundaries of what others consider normal work. The "overperformer" often threatens those who lack drive and ambition, and an effort must be made to avoid petty jealousy interfering with these performers.

PROCESS IMPROVEMENT

The management of the key processes of production is at the very heart of operations management. Managers need to examine how they are doing things and strive to find better ways. A beginning point in examining any process is to ask, "Why do we do it that way?" The response better not be, "Because we've always done it that way!" Process improvement should be an on-going exercise, not a program-of-the-month. A basic approach to the improvement of processes is:

1. Flowchart or diagram the process.
2. Walk through the process. The process is studied by following through all the steps of execution.
3. Interview the processors. Find out what they do and why they do it.
4. Streamline the process.

It helps to study similar processes at work in other organizations. Find out who does it best and either imitate them or surpass them.

Joseph Harrington, a manager with IBM, described his approach to process improvement in the book, *Business Process Improvement (1991)*. Harrington noted that an important step was to interview the people who work within the process. No one is more intimate with what they do and can have more ideas about better ways to do their work.

Harrington recommended the following questions:

- How were you trained?
- What do you do?
- How do you know your output is good?
- What feedback do you receive?
- Who are your customers?
- What keeps you from doing error-free work?
- What can be done to make your job easier?
- How is your output used?
- What would happen if you did not do the job?
- What would you change if you were the manager?

These questions help the analyst understand several things: the process itself, the culture of the workers involved in the process, and the management of the process workers. Deming's point about eliminating fear in the work place holds true for process improvements. There may be some hesitation on the part of the process workers to volunteer ways to improve their work, for they fear that they are putting themselves out of a job. If these fears can be alleviated, the workers will willingly offer their suggestions.

After the existing process is understood, it is time to find ways to improve the flow of the process. Harrington calls this "streamlining the process."

Streamlining the process

Harrington offered ten ways to make a process work better:

1. Bureaucracy Elimination—Remove unnecessary administrative tasks, approvals and paperwork.
2. Duplication Elimination—Remove identical activities.
3. Value-Added Assessment—Evaluate every activity to determine the contribution to meeting customer requirements. Real value-added activities are the ones customers will pay you to do.
4. Simplification—Reduce complexity.
5. Cycle-Time Reduction—Determine ways to compress time to meeting or exceeding customer requirements.
6. Error Proofing—Make the process difficult to do incorrectly.
7. Simple Language—Reduce the complexity of the way we write and talk.
8. Supplier Partnerships—Supplier input must improve.
9. Standardization—Do it the best way all the time.
10. Automation—Automate boring and routine activities.

Re-engineering

Michael Hammer and James Champy popularized the term "re-engineering," as a broader form of process improvement (1993). The term itself is not new, as Peter Drucker described "re-engineering" more than 20 years before Hammer and Champy. The concepts that Hammer and Champy espouse are not new either. What is new is the focus on process as a path for redirecting wayward companies. They defined re-engineering as "The fundamental rethinking and radical redesign of business processes to achieve dramatic improvements in critical, contemporary measures of performance, such as cost, quality, service, and speed." Hammer and Champy stress that re-engineering concerns reinvention, not improvement.

Although the many articles and books on quality and productivity have found an eager audience, the implementation of change must be done carefully, and when managers find themselves in crisis situations, it becomes an "all hands on deck" situation and all pretensions of bringing in new programs are discarded in favor of survival. The work force often suffers when one manager with a set of ideas is replaced by another with a different set of ideas. Constantly changing the processes can irritate the steady work force, who probably sighs and agrees to go with the flow until the next manager comes along with a set of new directions. Process changes will work best when the word "why?" floats throughout the corridors of a company. Change for the sake of change is not necessarily good. Change for the sake of advancement must be proved to those involved in the process.

Boeing was one company in need of a re-engineering effort. The company reduced its work force size by 10,000 in 1992 and anticipated cuts of 28,000 by 1994. While downsizing, efforts were underway to reduce the cycle-time of building a 737 from 13 months to six months. Boeing managers studied the production systems of several global manufacturing giants before outlining a training program designed to improve their processes.

General Motors found union resistance to their process improvement efforts and finally came to an agreement that United Auto Worker jobs would be saved if specific productivity targets were met.

The chief executive officer of Citicorp, John Reed, modeled the re-engineering of his bank after similar efforts at General Electric, Ford, and Cummins Engine Company. This example proves that service organizations can learn from process improvement efforts of manufacturers, and vice versa.

GLOBAL PRODUCTIVITY ISSUES

Despite the resurgence of quality in the world, examples of poor quality and poor customer service continue to abound. Many of the people reading this book have experienced the frustration of taking time off work to wait at home for some sort of service call: an appliance repair, the exterminator, etc. A customer calls an answering service and leaves a phone number; the call *may* be returned the next day. A day of service is selected, say Thursday afternoon, and not only do the service persons not arrive, but also do not notify the customer that they have unforeseen delays on other calls.

What can be more frustrating than leaving a car for scheduled repairs, only to return at the end of the day to learn that the shop was unable to work on the car because a certain part was unavailable. Stories are legion about quality improvements, but the fact remains that not every one receives the message and not every one cares.

No one intentionally wants to turn out something that is less than good. Deming puts the blame on management, insisting that 85 percent of quality problems are the fault of management and the system created by management.

Companies that have offices and plants around the world have to closely coordinate their measurement systems and process studies, sharing data, information, knowledge and skills, reward systems, and incentive packages.

The usual mechanism for plant informationsharing is an annual meeting of senior-level managers at the corporate headquarters. This is a good way to get together and share ideas and information. But, it should not stop there. When something is working exceptionally well at one plant or office, a number of managers at other locations should be brought in to study a successful system.

Cross-plant productivity comparisons should be analyzed carefully, since two plants may be operating under quite different constraints. It is demotivating to criticize a plant in one country for not meeting the standards of a plant in another country. Perhaps a more relevant comparison is drawn by comparing the productivity of a plant with its own performance in a prior period.

REFERENCES

Bowman, R. J. (1993). "Quality Management Comes to Global Transportation." *World Trade*, 6(2):38–40.

Bureau of Business Practice (1992). *Profile of ISO 9000*. Needham Heights, MA: Allyn & Bacon.

Charnes, A., W. W. Cooper, and E. Rhodes (1981). "Evaluating Program and Managerial Efficiency: an Application of Data Envelope Analysis to Program Follow-Through." *Management Science*, 27:668–697.

"Citicorp Chief Reed, Once A Big Thinker, Gets Down to Basics." *Wall Street Journal*, June 25, 1993, pp. 1, 4.

"GM Drive to Step Up Efficiency is Colliding with UAW Job Fears." *Wall Street Journal*, June 23, 1993, pp. 1, 8.

Garvin, D. A. (1992). *Operations Strategy*. Englewood Cliffs, NJ: Prentice-Hall.

Hammer, M. and J. Champy (1993). *Reengineering the Corporation*. New York: Harper Business.

Harrington, H. J. (1991). *Business Process Improvement*. McGraw-Hill.

Henkoff, R. "The Hot New Seal of Quality." *Fortune*, June 28, 1993, pp. 116–120.

Juran, J. M., F. M. Gryna, Jr., and R. S. Bingham, Jr. (eds.) (1988). *Quality Control Handbook*. New York: McGraw-Hill.

Sherman, H. D. (1984). "Improving the Productivity of Service Businesses." *Sloan Management Review*, 25:11–23.

Sink, D. S. (1985). *Productivity Management: Planning, Measurement and Evaluation Control and Improvement*. New York: John Wiley & Sons.

Young, S. T. (1992). "Multiple Productivity Measurement Approaches for Management." *Health Care Management Review*, 17(2):57–58.

5

Materials Management and Sourcing

The challenge of managing materials across plants and warehouses located in different countries and continents is to have inventory when you need it, but not until then. *Materials* management has always involved two basic policy decisions: (1) when to order, and (2) how much to order. Additional considerations include:

- What is the best inventory system to use?
- Do we deal with primary suppliers or multiple suppliers?
- Where do we store inventories?

Global firms can improve their materials management by networking inventory systems, connecting via electronic data interchange (EDI), and sharing a database of information. This chapter reviews the basic choices available and the basic principles of managing materials in global firms.

INVENTORY SYSTEMS

Basic configurations of inventory systems in use today include:

1. Independent demand inventory systems—usually used in retailing and wholesaling, hotels, and hospitals. These systems are only concerned with managing the inventory of the end product. Manufacturing firms with few parts may also find an independent demand system easier to manage than a dependent system.

2. Dependent demand inventory systems—used in assembly-type manufacturing. The prevailing form of this type of system is materials resource planning, commonly referred to as MRP II. In this system, orders for finished goods set in motion a "product explosion" that dictates the requirements for all parts included in the bill-of-materials for the product.
3. Just-in-time inventory systems—parts are delivered shortly before their actual use. Inventory levels are reduced to the absolute minimum.

Global inventory management must answer these key questions:

- Do we have a consortium of suppliers with the ability to deliver materials just-in-time?
- Do we have the capital to invest, or need to pursue, MRP software for inventory management?
- Can inventory be shared across plants/regions/countries?
- Do we have the software capabilities to access inventory information from a centralized database?

When to order?

The trigger for placing an order is the "reorder point," in an independent demand system. The reorder point is calculated by determining the expected demand during "lead time"—the time it takes from the point of realizing the need for a purchase to its actual receipt into inventory. For example, if it takes three days to receive flashlights and the demand is five a day, then the reorder point is 15. Since demand or lead time may vary, a safety stock is added to the reorder point. The safety stock is often calculated by multiplying the standard deviation of demand by a confidence factor from a Z statistic table. If a manager wanted to be 95 percent confident that she did not realize a stockout, she would look up the value for 95 percent on a Z table (1.65) and multiply that value by the standard deviation of demand.

Some managers may decide to simply add a couple or three days demand into the reorder point. This approach is probably more common.

MRP II systems trigger reorders by "exploding" the order for a finished product. In this process, customer orders determine the "gross requirements" for a product. All the inventory requirements for the parts that compose the product are determined by working backward from the end item's requirements through the cumulative lead times of the parts assembly and delivery.

JIT systems employ a "pull" philosophy—products are not built until they are ordered, therefore, orders pull the production system.

No matter what system is employed, the end goal is to maintain a product flow that meets demand.

How Much to Order?

The classical economic order quantity (EOQ) formula optimizes the quantity to purchase by accounting for all the costs of purchasing a good. The purchase order cost is the total labor cost of purchasing, receiving, and accounts payable, divided by the number of purchase orders placed per year (further divided by the average number of line items placed per order). The carrying cost is determined by multiplying the unit cost of an item by the percentage of carrying cost. The carrying cost percentage largely consists of the opportunity cost of capital: the current interest rate of a simple investment. In other words, if inventory was not in storage, the cash could be applied to an investment instrument that earns interest. Therefore, inventory involves a lost opportunity to earn interest on cash. Other inventory carrying costs include the cost of obsolescence, shrinkage, and the utilities cost for the warehouse.

The EOQ takes all of these costs into consideration and recommends the optimal purchase quantity. This assumes the firm has adequate cash flow and warehouse space. Managers may be startled to discover some EOQs involve the order of a six-month or more supply of a good, and the danger is that the dependence on the EOQ increases the probability of excessive quantities of obsolete inventory. Consequently, the primary managerial use of the EOQ is as an informational tool. Although it is the most famous of ordering formulas, it is not used by the majority of purchasing agents.

The emphasis in order strategies is to keep inventory lean, and turn the inventory frequently. This strategy enables the firm to be flexible to product demand changes.

ABC Analysis

Inventory expenditures tend to follow the Pareto principle—a few products are responsible for the greatest expenditures. This often takes the form of an inverse proportional arrangement, that is, 10 percent of the products take 70 percent of the expenditures, 70 percent of the products take 10 percent of the expenditures, with the other 20 percent of the products taking up the remaining 20 percent of the expenditures.

For example:

Table 5–1
ABC Analysis

Item Number	Annual Expenditure	% of Expenditure
19	54,000	27.0
24	48,000	24.0
41	38,000	19.0
90	21,000	10.5
75	10,000	5.0
98	6,000	3.0
93	4,000	2.0
15	3,000	1.5
5	3,000	1.5
51	3,000	1.5
74	2,000	1.0
67	2,000	1.0
36	2,000	1.0
4	1,000	0.5
54	1,000	0.5
95	1,000	0.5
7	1,000	0.5
46	400	0.2
96	300	0.15
70	300	0.15

An ABC inventory analysis requires the stratification of the inventory according to dollar expenditures. There is no one right way to stratify the inventory, but two popular stratifications are 70–20–10 and 80–10–10. A 70–20–10 stratification classifies the inventory so that the first 70 percent of dollar expenditures are classified as "A" items, the next 20 percent of expenditures are "B" items, and the last 10 percent are "C" items.

In the above example, assuming the classes are 70–20–10 and we establish a rule that items are classified as "A's" up to the first 70 percent of expenses. Items 19, 24, and 41 would then be classified as "A." These three items compose 70 percent of the total expenditures of all items. Item 90 falls into the "B" category, with item 75. The remaining 15 products make up the "C" category. So, in this hypothetical example, 15 percent of the products account for 70 percent of the expenditures, and 75 percent of the products account for 20 percent of the expenditures.

Inventory management can be streamlined by concentrating efforts on the "A" class. A greater proportion of time should be spent managing the "A's" than the rest of the inventory. The "A" class should be turned more frequently than the rest of the inventory, and more vigilance should be put into monitoring stock levels and demand changes. Since the greatest cost items are in the "A" class, it is a mistake to spend equal allocations of time toward the inventory (and purchasing) management of all items. A physical arrangement of stock according to class can also help focus efforts. By placing the highest cost items in a convenient, highly visible location, a materials manager can greatly reduce the time it takes to cycle count the inventory and make visual inspections of stock levels.

Inventory Accuracy

An important factor in effective inventory management is an accurate inventory system. Incorrect records can cause a manager to spend unusual amounts of time expediting materials. Or, it can cause unnecessary order placement.

A general rule-of-thumb is that the "A" items should be the most accurate of all inventory items. The American Production and Control Society (APICS) recommends that the inventory records of "A" items be approximately 99.5 percent, "B" items 99 percent, and "C" items 95 percent. These percentages do not appear difficult to achieve, but the fact is that many inventory record systems fall painfully shy of these standards.

A cycle count of inventory corrects inventory inaccuracies.

These counts are usually taken of a sample of inventory at periodic intervals (Young and Nie, 1992). However, cycle counts do not remedy inventory accuracy problems. Inventory inaccuracy should be treated as a quality management problem, with established control limits and methods of detection for problems.

A few causes of inventory inaccuracy are:

1. Unit-of-issue difference. Products may be received in cases of four boxes and then distributed in boxes. The failure to convert from cases to boxes could cause count errors.
2. Inventory is used without proper accounting. For example, a clerk fails to record the distribution of a box of copier paper to an office.
3. Inventory is lost, misplaced, or stolen.

Many firms rely on annual counts of physical inventory to update their inventory records. Periodic cycle counts benefit managers in providing early detection for inventory accuracy problems. A greater frequency of cycle counts helps reduce the record discrepancy that builds up over time. As the cycle counting frequency increases, the labor cost of cycle counting increases, stockouts decrease, and record accuracy increases. Chase and Aquilano (1992) advocated computer-generated notices alerting the need to cycle count. Ultimately, the choice of how frequently to cycle count is an economic decision. The total cost of inventory accuracy becomes the sum total of the cost of cycle counting and the cost of stockouts.

JIT

Toyota popularized the Just-in-time (JIT) inventory system with its "Kanban" system. Toyota managed its inventory using a method involving two Kanban cards, which were placed in buckets. Workers used a relay system to communicate their need for parts and parts were delivered exactly in the amount needed.

The Toyota system was simple and it worked. It was a variation of a commonly used inventory system called a "two-bin system," in which parts are pulled from a front storage bin, and a second bin's parts are pushed to the first bin, signaling the need to reorder. The real innovation of the Toyota system was going on at the receiving area of the plant. Toyota arranged for its suppliers to deliver parts shortly before they were actually used, requiring some suppliers to deliver more than once a day and many other suppliers to make daily deliveries. This changed the whole nature of the buyer-supplier relationship. Since the buyer of parts was so dependent on the delivery of parts by the supplier, the traditional adversarial relationship had to be dispensed. Suppliers became part of the firm.

Toyota realized very real cost advantages over other automobile manufacturers in the 1970s. They had little inventory, whereas their competition was bloated with inventories. At that time, their labor costs were much lower than their global competitors, although much of that advantage has diminished in the past 20 years.

The JIT system was used in most of Japan's leading manufacturers. Suppliers were located so they could meet the delivery cycles required of the manufacturers. Quality and productivity improved as inventories were reduced, and manufacturers across the world attempted to adopt the JIT philosophy. New automobile plants in the United States were all designed to use JIT, and it forced suppliers to change the way they did business.

Whether a company decides to go to a JIT system or not, the JIT sourcing philosophies apply to all organizations, although some governmental bodies and bureaucratically entangled companies may find implementation impossible. The move is on to reduce the supplier base. A philosophical shift has taken place—the old approach was to have multiple sources for a commodity, the new approach is to seek a primary source.

Here are some of the advantages and disadvantages of having a primary supplier:

Advantages

1. Reduced costs.
- Total purchasing costs are cut by negotiating better prices in exchange for promised orders.
- Reduced shipments cut freight costs paid by the buyer.
- Potential labor savings may lead to reduced personnel.
2. Reduced paperwork.
- Fewer invoices to process through accounts payable.
- Fewer purchase orders for purchasing.
- Fewer packing slips in receiving.
3. Time savings.
- Purchasing visits with fewer marketing representatives.
- Receiving handles fewer delivery trucks.
4. Better supplier relations.
- Getting to know the supplier's representative, customer service, and shipping employees better can lead to better relations.
5. Improved quality.
- Involving suppliers in the early stage of product design to incorporate quality into product and process designs.
- Providing technical support to suppliers to improve quality.

Disadvantages

1. The supplier may grow complacent after the contract is signed.
- Service may deteriorate and promises may not be delivered.
2. Lack of a competitive atmosphere leads to increased prices.
- The annual bidding process forces sellers to always keep their prices low.

The main reason to have multiple suppliers for a single commodity is to keep the suppliers on their competitive toes, forcing them to offer low prices to gain sales. The old way of buying was to solicit bids for commodities on an annual basis. The bids could be open, in which case the sellers were notified of the bid prices, or the bid could be sealed, in which case the bids are not revealed and the contract is awarded to a specific company. The U. S. government continues to operate on the annual bidding process.

The new approach to sourcing is to engage one supplier and commit to that one for a longer time period. In a JIT situation, the buyer is extremely dependent on the service of the supplier. A late delivery poses the potential to stop the line. This has actually changed the attitudes of companies on the social exchanges between their buyers and the suppliers. In the 1990s, a supplier is more like an employee of the buyer's company. They are helping the product or service to market, so they are part of the company, almost a member of the family. Trips to visit supplier plants are considered worthwhile. There are still boundaries of acceptable purchasing behavior that should never be violated, but all events that encourage superior buyer-seller relationships are encouraged.

In times when corporations must engage in cost-cutting to be competitive, suppliers are called on to sacrifice their share. In 1993, General Electric announced to its suppliers that they must cut their costs by 10 percent or lose GE's business.

General Motors' director of manufacturing in the 1980s and early 1990s, J. Ignacio Lopez, dispensed with efforts for long-term supplier relationships. Looking for ways to cut costs, he tore up many existing contracts and put the parts out for bid, showed suppliers blueprints from a competing supplier and asked them if they could do it better, and expected 20 percent price cuts across the board.

His strategy, called PICOS (purchased input concept optimization with suppliers), sent his own teams of engineers into supplier's plants to root out waste. A published article in BusinessWeek (August 31, 1992, p.29), said that "suppliers are more eager to deal with Toyota because of an atmosphere of trust." Also, " . . . Lopez, in his drive to yield immediate cost savings, has poisoned the atmosphere between GM and its suppliers."

Lopez ultimately departed for a key position with Volkswagen, but this is an example of the old-style relationships between buyers and suppliers.

Elements of JIT

In addition to the increased frequency of parts deliveries, the JIT system has several other features (Chase and Aquilano, 1992).

1. Focused factory networks.
2. Group technology.
3. Jidoka—quality at the source.
4. Uniform plant loading.
5. Minimized setup times.

Focused factories are small plants that concentrate on producing a narrow mix of products. At the plant level, this enables many efficiencies and savings through specialization of production. A network of such facilities enables a company to cover a broader range of products and manage overall organizational economies of scale.

Group technology (GT) is a facility layout that takes a U-shape and processes dissimilar parts with similar processing requirements. The GT layout is more common to Japanese manufacturers and is discussed at more length in the chapter, "Facility Location and Layout."

Jidoka is a Japanese philosophy of "quality at the source," which basically means that production is stopped when defects are detected. Other production systems are concerned with keeping the machines running at all times, and if defects are detected, they are pulled from the line, which never stops. The jidoka concept requires line workers to stop the line when they find defects, follow the defect to its source, correct the problem, and then turn the line back on. It is the preferred approach of quality-minded manufacturing managers.

The uniform plant loading philosophy concentrates on the production of the quantity needed each day, not the rate of the machinery. A JIT system builds products for actual orders, not to increase stock. Then, a monthly production schedule is established, scheduling a mix of products that protects them in cases of schedule variation.

The JIT production system must have smaller lot sizes, necessitating that machine setup times be minimal. Managers faced with minimizing setup times must find a variety of time-saving methods to accomplish these times.

Beyond production practices, the Japanese JIT system had decidedly different labor-management relations, which helped the system work. An integral practice was participative management. Workers at all levels of the organization were empowered to make decisions, to make suggestions that were actually heeded. Quality circles succeeded in Japan because management authentically listened to the ideas of the work force, and workers knew that many of their ideas were implemented.

In many of the larger Japanese corporations, lifetime employment was assured for workers and managers. This created a strong feeling of worker identity to the employer, such that one line worker, pulled from the line and asked his name, was said to have replied, "I am Toyota!"

William Ouchi, in his book, "Theory Z," wrote that the American organization that most resembled the Japanese organization was the United States military (1981). The U.S. military considered the family units of military personnel as part of a great, big defense family. Since personnel are frequently moved across the world, the military took care of the needs of the spouses and children of its work force.

The systems of jidoka, group technology, faster setups, and participative management will not work unless the management system is in place that allows its workers to help make their own work flow better.

The Bose Corporation, a manufacturer of stereo components, initiated a system they call, "JIT II." In JIT II, a supplier representative places orders and has an office in the Bose plant, encouraging frequent supplier-buyer interchange. Bose has found the JIT II system very successful in reducing purchasing personnel and inventory.

Where to Source?

There is no simple answer to the question of where to buy. The primary criteria should be:

1. Total cost.
2. Quality.
3. Customer service.
4. Responsiveness.
5. Delivery capabilities.

Some managers have gone so far as to develop a qualitative assessment technique, similar to the productivity measurement approach (MCP/PMT) discussed in Chapter 4.

One question is, "If the product is available through a local vendor at a higher price, should I purchase from them to contribute to the local economy?" The answer is, "Only if the higher price is offset by superior delivery, quality, and customer service." Otherwise, your contribution to the local economy is zero, because the price difference is money lost in profit from your company. There may be other occasions where you will decide to purchase from a local, higher priced source, and they may include:

1. The speed and convenience of local delivery outweighs all other decision factors.
2. There is some sort of a vertical integration or collaborative partnership arrangement with the seller.
3. A member of your family works for the seller.

The third factor here, of course, is not appropriate to this decision. However, it may very well be a factor such as this that sways the buyer.

ETHICS IN GLOBAL BUYING

Operations managers must realize that they cannot afford to be naive when it comes to the potential for graft and corruption surrounding buyer-seller relationships. In a high-pressure, competitive sales environment, incentives are frequently tossed at buyers that violate ethical standards. These may be in the form of gifts, vacations, cash, or even sex.

It is said that sellers, similarly, cannot afford to deal in a business world unwary of the possibility of corrupt buyers. To protect themselves, many marketing people feel they must discover whether or not they must offer some sort of incentive to a purchasing agent to seal a deal.

In some countries, what we in the United States call bribery is considered to be no more than the cost of doing business. Some American companies complain that they lost business because of American laws that prohibit "bribery," causing them to lose business to corporations from other nations. The customary practice is to account for such practices as "consulting fees." It is sad, but true, that some international bids are settled by the company with the most to offer in financial incentives to buyers.

Assuming an ethical world, with upright, moral buyers, the most important sourcing consideration for operations is the receipt of raw materials in a timely manner.

COUNTERTRADE

In some scenarios, countertrade is employed in exchange for raw materials. Countertrade is an arrangement in which the sale of goods and services is linked to an import purchase of other goods and services. Angelidis (1989) outlined the major forms of countertrade:

1. Barter—the oldest form of countertrade. Seller and buyer exchange goods and services, but not money.
2. Counterpurchase—requires two contracts. Import firm Y in country Y purchases goods or services from export firm X in country X, and import firm X in country X also purchases goods or services from firm Y, but the contracts are made independently.
3. Reverse countertrade—an advance purchase is made against a future counterpurchase obligation.
4. Compensation/buyback—the seller builds a facility in the purchasing country and buys back an agreed percentage of the output of the facility.

Countertrade, a tool that buyers and sellers of the 1990s must understand in global markets, brings a new dimension to the negotiation skills of a buyer. The buyer must have a keen sense of value when approaching the negotiating table in a countertrade transaction.

Materials management is one of the most important functions of operations management. It is an area of the firm in which good performance is assumed, and the presence of the managers is often neglected until there is some sort of miscue. However, as much as 25 to 40 percent of a firm's costs are at stake in materials, and effective management can realize tremendous cost savings. Conversely, if it is not being well managed, it can be the biggest headache in the world and cause lost customers.

The keys to cross-plant materials management are coordination and communication. The avoidance of duplicate inventories, quick response to changes in demand patterns, and elimination of obsolete inventory are elementary managerial actions that good materials managers practice and the not-so-good don't.

TECHNOLOGY IN MATERIALS MANAGEMENT

Electronic data interchange (EDI), an electronic link between buyer and supplier, enables the buyer to access the warehouse computer of a supplier and determine availability and price of a commodity. This has become standard industry technology. Volvo, for example, reduced inventories 67 percent by using EDI to transmit delivery schedules, dispatch notices, invoices, and other documents (Forger, 1991). EDI and bar coding technology were major factors in Volvo's productivity improvements.

Other warehouse technologies found to improve productivity in materials management include automated materials handling systems and pick-to-light picking systems, in which stock pickers pick needed stock though a warehouse lighting system (Forger, 1993).

REFERENCES

Angelidis, J. (1989). *Countertrade*. (Unpublished dissertation.) Atlanta: Georgia State University.

Business Week, August 31, 1992, p. 29.

Chase, R., and N. Aquilano (1992). *Production and Operations Management*. Homewood, IL: Irwin.

Forger, G. (1991). "Making Bar Code Labels and EDI Pay off." *Modern Materials Handling*, 46(7):57–59.

Forger, G. (1993). "Warehouse Upgrade Records a 30% Efficiency Gain." *Modern Materials Handling*, 48(10):38–40.

Ouchi, W. (1981). *Theory Z*. New York: Addison-Wesley.

Young, S. T. and W. Nie (1992). "A Cycle Count Model Considering Inventory Policy and Record Variance." *Production and Inventory Management Journal*, First Quarter: 11–16.

6

Facility Location and Layout

Two of the most important and basic factors to achieving global operations management success are the choice of an effective facility location and layout. Where do we locate our plants and headquarters? How do we layout the production process within the plant? These may be the most critical of all operations considerations.

Assembly manufacturing has perhaps the most complex set of location decisions. Where do we assemble the major components of our product? Do we assemble everything in one location, or is it advantageous to pass the various stages of assembly to plants across the globe?

This chapter will look at the basic configurations of location and layout. We will discuss the practical considerations of effective decisions in this area and present a number of quantitative and qualitative approaches to these decisions.

LOCATION

Real estate agents will tell you that the three most important factors in determining a house's value are "location, location, and location." Service organizations that locate to serve a local client base know that location is probably the number one determinant of revenue. Manufacturing firms that ship across the globe are less constrained by location and can learn to maneuver around existing transportation and shipping networks.

There are four ways that an initial location decision is made:

1. A quantitative model determines the optimal location, considering a number of quantified factors.
2. A qualitative model determines the optimal location, considering a number of subjective and quantified factors.
3. A cost-benefit approach determines the least-cost location.
4. Executive amenities are the strongest consideration.

Academics spend many hours teaching business students the first three approaches, although the fourth approach is sometimes the determining factor.

We will address all of these approaches for services and manufacturing firms.

Quantitative Models

A number of academic disciplines, including real estate, operations management, industrial engineering, accounting, and geography, have explored a vast array of approaches to the location problem. Some of these result in statistical models, others in linear programming formulations, still others in heuristic algorithms of some sort.

Brandeau and Chiu (1989) did an extensive literature review of the approaches to the location problem. They classified these approaches into three primary methods:

   I. Exact Solution Techniques
      A. Analytical Solution/Optimality Result
      B. Integer Programming/Branch and Bound
      C. Dynamic Programming/Backtrack Programming
      D. Convex Programming
      E. Other
  II. Heuristic Solution Techniques
      A. Exchange Heuristics
      B. Greedy Heuristics
      C. Drop Heuristics
      D. Sequential Location and Allocation
      E. Solution of an Approximate Problem
      F. Solution of a Relaxed Problem
      G. Solution of a Restricted Problem
      H. Other
 III. Techniques for Evaluation of heuristics
      A. Bound on Optimal Solution
      B. Worst Case Solution

C. Probabalistic Analysis
D. Statistical Evaluation
E. Stopping Rule

(Source: Brandeau, M. and S. Chiu, "An Overview of Representative Problems," *Management Science*, 35(6):665, 1989)

Typical criteria for selecting a "best" method might include the minimum travel time or the minimum costs. Typical problems might be:

1. Where do we locate a warehouse that will receive parts from existing plants?
2. Where do we locate a new manufacturing plant, given the location of our existing plants, customers, and competition?
3. Where do we locate a service (such as a hotel, restaurant, hospital, or auto repair shop) given customers, demographic trends, traffic patterns, and existing competition?
4. Which plants do we close, given changes in product demand, existing customers, and competition?
5. How many regional headquarters do we need, and where should they be?

Gravity Methods

The center of gravity method is one type of location approach. It considers existing locations and might be applied to a scenario in which the new facility will ship to a number of pre-existing sites. For example, let us assume we are to build a warehouse to serve five department stores in greater Salt Lake City, Utah. We need to know the map coordinates of the existing stores, plus the shipping costs to the new facility. Costs are determined by the number of units shipped times the per-unit shipping cost.

A coordinate grid map must be drawn, selecting an arbitrary point to serve as the (0,0) axis at the intersection of the X and Y coordinates.

Therefore, the X,Y center of gravity, considering the cost of shipping, is at location X = 3.4, Y = 34. Since the Y axis represents U.S. Interstate 15 in this example, this will place the recommended site for a new warehouse 3.4 miles east of the interstate and 34 miles north of the arbitrary axis.

Once the center of gravity is found, the search for a site involves numerous factors.

After a country location has been decided upon, Great Britain, for example, the process shifts focus to regions within a country, that is, Scotland, Northern Ireland, Western England, etc.

Table 6–1
Location Analysis

Existing Sites	(X) Units		Ship Cost	Total Cost
Provo	5	900	$1	$4,500
Sandy	1	600	1	600
SLC1	8	400	1	3,200
SLC2	1	1200	1	1,200
Ogden	5	700	1	3,500
Units		3800	Total Cost	13,000

Center (X) = 13,000/3800 = 3.4

Existing Sites	(Y) Units		Ship Cost	Total Cost
Provo	0	900	$1	$0
Sandy	20	600	1	12,000
SLC1	35	400	1	14,000
SLC2	40	1200	1	48,000
Ogden	80	700	1	56,000
Units		3800	Total Cost	130,000

Center (Y) = 130,000/3800 = 34

Table 6–2
Factors in Site Location

Regional	City	Site
Market potential	Market potential	Land price
Transportation	Transportation	Transportation
Raw materials	Raw materials	Zoning ordinances
State taxes	Local taxes	Physical characteristics
Labor costs	Labor costs	Local amenities
Labor availability	Labor availability	Local housing
Labor skills	Labor skills	Utilities
Other incentives	Other incentives	Local services

If the focus shifts to Scotland for reasons of available labor and a favorable transportation system, then the decision centers on a specific city. The site selection process usually takes place before the city is announced, to make certain of the availability of desirable locations within a city.

The Mercedes-Benz decision to locate in Alabama in the United States is a good example ("Why Mercedes is Alabama Bound," *BusinessWeek*, October 11, 1993, pp.138–139.). Mercedes decided to build a plant for a new multipassenger vehicle. Mercedes' management believed that the greatest market for this car was in the United States, considering the combined costs of labor, shipping, components, and currency swings. They originally selected 100 sites in 35 states from California to the East Coast.

These sites were narrowed further after considering transportation costs and the age distribution and mix of skilled and semiskilled workers. A site selection team worked in secret, to avoid the circus atmosphere surrounding most major location decisions. When the media discover their city is a possible target for a new plant site, they write articles and broadcast news reports, causing the expectations of the citizens to rise, and the companies are besieged by politicians, celebrities, and the like, trying to persuade them to come to their city.

After eight months of searching and analysis, Mercedes announced three finalists in the United States: Alabama, North Carolina, and South Carolina. Alabama won after promising more than $200 million in job training, tax breaks, and other incentives. Mercedes officials said that the long-term costs of the three locations were not far apart, but they were impressed by Alabama's determination to win the award. They also felt comfortable in Alabama, remarking that the site featured wooded, rolling hills, similar to the countryside outside of Stuttgart.

Certain location decisions require extra attention to ward off potential problems. Faced with the perception of poor quality and service from Mexican plants, General Motors located a plant in Mexico and was extremely vigilant about maintaining plant quality by making weekly phone contact with customers to understand their requirements and holding monthly person-to-person meetings (Toledano, 1993).

Chinese manufacturing has a reputation of having insufficient managerial talent, and quality problems (Engen, 1994). The Loctite Corporation delayed opening a Chinese plant until a Chinese management team could be trained in the company's style.

The Factor Rating Method

A simple, qualitative approach to facility location is to assign weighted scores to a number of important factors. For example, a company in need of a new manufacturing plant has narrowed its choices to Dublin, Ireland and Tours, France, and the important criteria for this decision are labor costs, estimated fixed costs, access to customers, transportation access, and availability of raw materials. Each criterion is assigned a weight according to importance, and a score for each city, with 5 being the best and 1 the worst. (The scoring system is totally arbitrary.) The score might work out something like this:

Table 6–3
Factor Rating Method

	Dublin	Tours
Labor costs (.3)	4	3
Est. fixed costs (.3)	4	2
Customer access (.2)	1	1
Transportation (.1)	2	2
Raw materials (.1)	1	1
Total score	2.9	2.0

The score is the summation of the criteria weight times each score. This is not exactly the most scientific approach to location selection, but may ultimately be as effective as some of the mathematical models. Good information and good accounting data are absolute essentials for any location decision.

In the United States, a helpful source of city data is *The Places Rated Almanac* (1994), which applies the factor rating method to its determination of the best cities to live in. Since factors that make a city desirable to live in are often identical to the factors for choosing a plant or headquarters location, this book is a good reference. One location strategy in recent years is to locate in remote, sparsely-populated locales where unemployment is high. This strategy is to find a place less likely to unionize, since people are happy to have good-paying jobs. Also, it puts the company in a situation where it is less likely to lose skilled employees. In large population centers with heavy manufacturing concentrations, such as Detroit, Chicago, and Pittsburgh, it is possible for employees to find other employment on their lunch breaks. This is not very possible in places like Smyrna, Tennessee (Nissan) or Normal, Illinois (Mitsubishi).

The Places Rated Almanac rates cities in nine categories: Cost of living, jobs, crime, health care and environment, transportation, education, the arts, recreation, and climate. Each category has a number of considerations that make up the total score. In one category, jobs, the score was determined by two factors: the total number of forecasted jobs and the percentage rate of job growth.

After all factors were put together and equally weighted, Cincinnati came out as the best city in which to live in the United States.

BEST CITIES FOR BUSINESS

Fortune magazine annually ranks the best cities for business, on the basis of surveys of nearly 1,000 corporate executives in America's 60

Table 6–4
America's Top 25 Metropolitan Areas (1989 vs. 1993)

1993	(1989)
1. Cincinnati, Ohio	(14)
2. Seattle, Washington	(1)
3. Philadelphia, Pennsylvania	(13)
4. Pittsburgh, Pennsylvania	(3)
5. Raleigh-Durham, North Carolina	(23)
6. Washington, D.C.	(4)
7. Indianapolis, Indiana	(30)
8. Salt Lake City, Utah	(16)
9. Louisville, Kentucky	(9)
10. Atlanta, Georgia	(11)
11. Portland, Oregon	(24)
12. Knoxville, Tennessee	(35)
12. Cleveland, Ohio	(12)
14. San Diego, California	(5)
15. Boston, Massachusetts	(6)
16. San Francisco, California	(2)
16. Greensboro–Winston-Salem, North Carolina	(62)
18. Syracuse, New York	(21)
19. Baltimore, Maryland	(17)
20. St. Louis, Missouri	(29)
21. Orange County, California	(8)
22. Detroit, Michigan	(53)
23. Eugene-Springfield, Oregon	(38)
24. Oklahoma City, Oklahoma	(49)
25. Los Angeles, California	(15)

largest areas ("The Best Cities for Knowledge Workers," *Fortune*, November 15, 1993, pp. 50–78). In 1993, *Fortune* ranked the top ten cities for knowledge workers as:

1. Raleigh/Durham
2. New York City
3. Boston
4. Seattle
5. Austin
6. Chicago
7. Houston

8. San Jose
9. Philadelphia
10. Minneapolis

SERVICE LOCATIONS

Service location decisions consider customer demographics, traffic patterns, labor cost and availability, and real estate costs among the primary factors. Service organizations are more prone to using statistical models, and franchises with many established units are able to predict the success of a new unit by plugging in values to a model on the basis of previous experience.

One example of the building of a service model is given by Sheryl E. Kimes and James A. Fitzsimmons (1990). Kimes and Fitzsimmons built a regression model to predict profitable new sites. They determined that the best dependent variable was operating margin, since the occupancy rate did not necessarily indicate profitability. Kimes and Fitzsimmons discovered that the importance of the independent variables changed over time. In 1986, profitable sites had more nearby college students, military bases, hospital beds, and office space. However, the important independent variables changed in later years.

GEOGRAPHIC INFORMATION SYSTEMS

A technology that has quickly become the tool of choice for location planners is geographic information systems (GIS). GIS is a software package that includes digitized maps and demographic data ("Mapping for Dollars," *Fortune*, 10/18/93, pp. 91–96.). Optical scanners are used to trace existing maps to add to the software.

GIS allows the analyst to overlay demographic data, providing a visual inspection of areas of interest. For example, a manager may want to know the postal code with the highest concentration of Catholics, an average household income exceeding $80,000, and the fewest ice cream stores per capita. The GIS would overlay these demographics to highlight the area for a possible new Catholic ice cream store.

The leading software producers of GIS include Strategic Mapping of Santa Clara, California, MapInfo of Troy, New York, and Tactics International of Andover, Massachusetts. These systems have been employed by such firms as Yellow Freight, for delivery routes; Norwest Corporation, a bank analyzing the sources of their loan customers; and Cigna, for locations of Cigna-affiliated physicians.

The combination of statistical, graphical, and visual analysis offered to managers has resulted in the popularization of GIS at the expense of the mathematical models.

EXECUTIVE WHIM

The reality of location decisions often is that the executive suite picks a location for personal reasons. There are more accounts of this method of location selection than any other.

The state of Florida in the United States has proved to be a popular place to locate a plant or headquarters, and the Florida Office of Economic Development knows how to sell the state. The location decision-makers are often males in their mid-fifties and older. If their company is interested in Florida as a potential site, these managers are certain to get a tour that will include golf courses. The state of Florida is appealing to executives approaching retirement because there are no state income taxes and retiree dollars go farther.

Utah, Colorado, Wyoming, Montana, Idaho, Eastern California, New Mexico, and the Northeastern states can sell skiing to executives who find mountain living to their liking. Executives who choose locations to pursue their personal hobbies may not be doing such a bad thing. In many ways, a company that evolves around a certain sport, be it skiing, golf, or cricket, may have a culture in place that thrives in a location where they can do their thing more often.

LOCATION WAR STORIES

AM International was a company victimized by executive whim. They hired a CEO who decided the company had a stodgy image and that Cleveland was the wrong place for a new image. So, he began his transformation of AM by moving the company to Los Angeles, changing the company name, and buying up new high-tech companies while divesting AM of their low-tech businesses. This CEO was fired after about a year on the job. The next CEO believed his predecessor had made some strategic mistakes, and moved the company headquarters to *his* hometown, Chicago. Then, *he* quit after only seven months on the job. Imagine how the managers and families of AM employees felt after two moves in two years.

Another well-known tale of location decision-making was chronicled in *Barbarians at the Gate* (1990). Ross Johnson, the CEO of Reynolds-Nabisco, was unhappy living in conservative Winston-Salem, North Carolina. Johnson's wife, a svelte and tan woman 20 years his junior, was not greeted with open arms by the Winston-Salem country club set.

Perhaps the wives of the Reynolds executives were afraid their husbands would want to trade them in on a model like Mrs. Johnson. In any event, the Johnsons didn't fit in Winston-Salem, so he moved the headquarters to Atlanta, leaving vacant a $25 million dollar office building and a town built by Reynolds Tobacco. Stories like this are frustrating to those who advocate well-researched and thoughtful location decisions, but they happen all the same.

THE "HOLLOW" CORPORATION

An issue that is part a sourcing issue and part a location issue is whether to produce off-shore, that is, in another country, to realize labor cost advantages. Korea, Taiwan, and Mexico are three countries where companies have sought cheaper labor for lower-skilled manufacturing work. In some cases, companies totally subcontract *all* of their manufacturing to a number of plants across the world. Nike, for example, does none of its manufacturing in the United States, choosing instead to subcontract and position key managers in the subcontractor plants to assure quality.

"Hollowing out" has become a controversial topic and some say that the overemphasis on off-shore manufacturing has weakened the manufacturing base of the United States, thus weakening the U.S. economy overall. The major disadvantage in off-shore manufacturing is in not locating closer to customers who then choose to deal with closer producers. However, many customers do not care at all whether a product is made in Mexico or the Philippines, as long as they can have it when they want it.

FACILITY LAYOUT

Essential to productivity and quality is an effective facility layout. The major classes of layout are *product and process layouts*. A *product* layout, exemplified by the assembly line, typically moves a product through a sequential series of steps to complete production. The assembly line has advantages in streamlining production, but disadvantages in the sociological and psychological aspects of the line on the worker. Repetitive work can lead to job dissatisfaction, so workers in assembly lines are prime candidates for job enrichment efforts. It is generally accepted that workers would prefer variety over routine in their daily tasks, but that is not always the case. Range Rover in England has discovered that its senior workers, who have the choice of which tasks they perform, prefer to do one simple task repeatedly, rather than complicate things with a number of other duties.

Volvo introduced a new concept to auto manufacturing in its Uddevalla, Sweden plant ("Volvo's Radical New Plant: 'The Death of the Assembly Line'," *BusinessWeek*, August 28, 1989, pp. 92–94). Teams of seven to ten hourly workers assembled one car per shift. Volvo claimed that this method produced cars with fewer hours of labor than its other plants and realized major reductions in absenteeism. Although this concept was introduced in 1987, there was not a stampede of imitators at Volvo's heels, and Volvo ultimately scrapped the project.

The team approach to automobile production eliminated the negatives of the assembly line. Being responsible for the entire production of an auto helps bring more of a feeling of ownership to the worker. In Ben Hamper's book, *Rivethead* (1986), he noted how the only time the workers seemed to feel anything toward their product was the day they were told one of the Suburbans was being built for the country singer Barbara Mandrell. Assembly line workers are so removed from customers that they lose sight of their contribution to production.

Process Layouts

Process layouts are also called "job shops," layouts in which areas of the company involve different processes. One example of a process layout is a hospital, which includes such processes as emergencies, intensive care, surgeries, labor and delivery, and respiratory therapy in treating patients. Another example is a print shop that has areas for copying, binding, color copying, and self-service printing.

In laying out a process configuration, the idea is to minimize the cost of the flow of goods among the various departments or areas. A load-distance chart reveals the cost of moving a unit of product times the distance between two departments. For example:

It costs $25 (assuming $1 per unit times a distance measured as 25 unit-distances) to move from A to B, $65 to move from A to C, and $80 from B to C.

An initial matrix for all combinations of interdepartmental product moves is derived, and improvements are made to minimize the total cost of all movements. The first computer program developed to handle

Table 6–5
Process Layout Matrix

	A	B	C
A	-	25	65
B	-	-	80
C	-	-	-

this problem was Computerized Relative Allocation of Facilities Technique (CRAFT), developed by Armour and Buffa. CRAFT executed pairwise-exchanges of areas until no cost improvements are found. Other computer programs attempting process layout improvements are ALDEP, COFAD, CORELAP, and PLANET.

These computer programs are helpful but do not consider human and other practical considerations that must later be made.

Group Technology

A popular layout since the 1980s is *cellular manufacturing,* or *group technology.* In this type of layout, dissimilar machines are grouped according to similar processing requirements. These machines are grouped in U-shaped cells. Cellular layouts have been found to have shorter setup times, lower machine utilization and shorter distance traveled than conventional process layouts.

Flexible Manufacturing Systems (FMS)

Flexible manufacturing systems (FMS) are unmanned systems that include machining centers, automated materials handling systems, a robot, a storage rack, and loading and unloading stations. The increased flexibility these systems offer for changing product mixes have attracted manufacturers across the world. These expensive systems have found their greatest popularity in Germany and Japan.

CONCLUSIONS

Location and layout decisions are two of the most strategic areas in all of global operations management. While many mathematical models are developed to handle these problems, these decisions are usually made for reasons that have little to do with math. The effectiveness and zeal of the governmental offices that market the attractiveness of a certain country are often the determining factor for location decisions.

The work of the management scientists, industrial engineers, accountants, and operations managers in analyzing various locations and layouts should be considered, certainly. So, too, must cultural factors, skill levels, access to customers, and distance from competition. We may scoff at skiing, golf, and other executive interests as reasons to locate, but we cannot argue against these seemingly arbitrary decisions as perhaps being a part of the culture which makes a company tick.

REFERENCES

"The Best Cities for Knowledge Workers." *Fortune*, November 15, 1993, pp. 50–78.

Boyer, R., and D. Savageau (1989). *Places Rated Almanac*. (Englewood Cliffs, NJ: Prentice-Hall.

Brandeau, M., and S. Chiu (1989). "An Overview of Representative Problems." *Management Science*, 35(6):665.

Burroughs, B. and J. Helyar (1990). *Barbarians at the Gate*. New York: Harper & Row.

Engen, J. R. (1994). "Getting Your Chinese Workforce Up to Speed." *International Business*, 7(8):44–48.

Hamper, B. (1986). *Rivethead*. New York: Warner Books.

Kimes, S. E. and J. A. Fitzsimmons (1990). "Selecting Profitable Hotel Sites at La Quinta Motor Inns." *Interfaces*, 20(2):12–20.

"Mapping for Dollars," *Fortune*, October 18, 1993, pp. 91–96.

Savageau, D., and R. Boyer (1994). *Places Rated Almanac*. Englewood Cliffs, NJ: Prentice-Hall.

"Why Mercedes is Alabama Bound." *BusinessWeek*, October 11, 1993, pp. 138–139.

Toledano, S. H. (1993). "Mexican Location Considerations." *Business Mexico*, 3(4):11–14.

"Volvo's Radical New Plant: 'The Death of the Assembly Line.'" *BusinessWeek*, August 28, 1989, pp. 92–94.

7

Managing Human Resources in Global Operations

Ultimately, operations success is a function of the people who work for a company. In Hayes, Wheelwright, and Clark's book, *Dynamic Manufacturing* (1988), one of their concluding themes was that in excellent manufacturing companies, "management makes the difference." This almost sounds like a flippant remark. "Of course, management makes a difference!" might be the reply of the casual business observer. Yet, Hayes, Wheelwright, and Clark found demonstrable differences when studying a number of plants. Within any one industry, there are firms that execute their operational plans to perfection and have visibly well-oiled production machines operating with little waste. Meanwhile, another firm within that same industry may be operating without any semblance of a plan and have a system that reflects the lack of planning—dirt, noise, and waste are everywhere. Many firms lack the commitment to do the hard work that it takes to achieve excellence.

A wonderfully designed and innovative product that customers love and buy by the billions is not enough to sustain a company for more than a generation. Products are duplicated and copied eventually. Everyone achieves high quality. How well a company performs long-term is going to be largely determined by its management system.

The people of the company are, without a doubt, the greatest asset, and this asset is not inventoried. When the annual physical count of everything the company owns is tallied, no one takes a piece of paper and says, "Let's see, Joe knows this, and Sally knows that, and Jeanne has this skill, and Mohammed has that skill . . . " The real goal of top management should be to increase the value of that hidden asset.

Experienced managers know that human relations is a very real part of human resource management, and many managers have learned this in the form of a painful lesson. Managers often make mistakes in human relations. The important thing is to learn from those mistakes and not make them again.

This chapter focuses on ways to increase the value of this hidden asset. The topics covered include:

- Training and development.
- Compensation and incentive systems.
- Motivation.
- Improving the quality of work life.
- Recruitment and selection.
- Labor relations.
- Performance evaluation.
- Women in the operations work force.
- Environmental concerns.
- Cultural considerations

TRAINING AND DEVELOPMENT

Employee knowledge and skills are built through the training and development of employees. Large corporations enjoy the benefit of training and development staffs, fully equipped with fine facilities and classrooms superior to the facilities of the finest business schools. Many of the trainers on these staffs have Ph.D.'s in either business or education. Some training is also subcontracted to consultants or university professors.

Employees need several types of training:

1. Specific position–oriented training.
2. Specific skill–based training.
3. Management development.
4. Employee development.
5. Team-building seminars.
6. Quality-oriented training.
7. Remedial mathematics and languages classes.
8. Foreign language training.
9. Corporate culture orientations.
10. Human development training.

In addition to on-site training, employees should have the opportunity to further their educational background with company support.

This may be to complete a high school education, college, or graduate program. Some firms only reimburse tuition if the classes are job-specific. However, *all* education makes the employee a more well-rounded and loyal individual. Even a college class in country line-dancing can be justified, because it may open up more social opportunities for the individual, thus improving their quality of life.

The cost of paying for all this training is the inhibiting factor in considering how far to go with tuition-reimbursement plans. Obviously, it is difficult to pay industry-standard wages and include this employee benefit unless the firm is profitable. Tuition reimbursement should be part of an employment contract that specifies that the beneficiary of training will not leave the employer for a suitable period after receiving the education. Referring back to Deming's quality cycle—if excellent, quality products and services are sent to market, the company will be more profitable. Training and personal development contribute to a strongly motivated workforce that can help achieve quality and profitability. If you know more than the competition and have better skills, you will lead the market, assuming the product is of industry-standard.

All classes in personal development benefit the employer. Classes in such areas as improving negotiation skills, memory skills, personal fitness, and personal financial planning serve to challenge the employee and further their problem-solving skills.

When firms suffer through hard economic times, the first place budgets are cut is often training and development. This should be the last place, since cutting training is akin to sacrificing the future. An important part of development is knowing current and future trends within job specialties, information that can be garnered from trips to seminars, annual conventions, and trade shows. The benefit of these sojourns is that the employees rub elbows with people who have similar problems at their own work places, and much can be learned from them. One consideration for economizing on travel might be to pay for an expert to speak at the company headquarters, rather than sending a number of employees away to hear the speaker.

How does a company measure the effectiveness of training and development? Senior managers may not accept the answer that it is measured by the bottom line. Periodic surveys of employee satisfaction are one approach. These surveys should correlate satisfaction with company dollars spent on education, training, and development. Employees should be surveyed on completion of their training. Did they enjoy the course? Will it help them at work? Was the instructor effective? Did they learn anything new? Did they learn anything that could result in improved performance at work? Finally, overall studies of employee attendance, turnover, and productivity should be gauged against the costs of training and development.

Small businesses do not enjoy the luxury of large budgets to increase the knowledge base of their workforce. To survive financially, small businesses should do all they possibly can to improve their employees' knowledge or risk losing motivated employees to more educationally-minded firms.

Global firms must maintain a database management system that tracks the training efforts of all plants and headquarters. A coordinated effort in all training and development activities can avoid redundant training. For example, one site may contract for an outside consultant to train in TQM, only to discover that an expert was available at another site within the company. Although employee knowledge cannot be inventoried, the list of training programs attended should be tracked.

Companies that have a global workforce need also pay attention to cultural and language improvement seminars. If employees are sent around the world, advance preparation in the customs and living standards of the foreign country is helpful in improving that employee's chance of success in a foreign environment.

COMPENSATION AND REWARD SYSTEMS

The most serious compensation problem is the overcompensation of many senior executives. The inequity between senior executive pay and the rest of the workforce is perpetuated by a system in which a board, comprised largely of other CEOs, awards CEO salaries exceeding one million U.S. dollars. This practice is demotivating to the workforce. Those that defend this practice use the same argument that is used to defend the need for a monarchy—the people need a symbol of leadership, and the rewards of making it to the top of the company should come with visible financial and material benefits. Operations managers dealing with line workers must face motivating a disillusioned, dissatisfied workforce when the workers' jobs are being cut, while the senior management team is awarded with cash bonuses.

Another compensation problem is the long-term impact of rewarding short-term financial performance. Managers compensated with bonuses according to their performance toward the annual bottom line often tend to postpone needed expenditures for capital improvements in the firm. Because these managers look good on paper for several years, they eventually get promoted and the buck passes to their successors who are ultimately left with an outdated plant.

David Cherrington (1991) wrote that pay should achieve six objectives. Pay should:

1. Be legal.
2. Be adequate.
3. Be motivating.
4. Be equitable.
5. Provide security.
6. Be cost-benefit effective.

Employees must feel that they are being paid a fair wage for their services. Local markets are the biggest determinant of equity. An employee in Tibet doing the same job for the same company as an employee in Boston may be paid $5 per hour less. The cost of living, the replacement cost of hiring and firing, and the availability of qualified labor factor into fair compensation. Within local markets, companies must maintain equitable pay according to job class and tenure with the company.

Global companies with production plants across the world may encounter forms of racial and gender discrimination in the local compensation and hiring practices. Although discrimination may be the norm in a certain region, the ethical practice is to maintain equity at your own house and advocate reforms in these unenlightened regions.

A number of incentive plans have been invented over the years, including Scanlon plans, Gainsharing, stock option plans and profit sharing. These plans were designed to trade increased pay for increased productivity. One author, Alfred Kohn, ("Why Incentive Plans Cannot Work," *HBR*, Vol. 71, No. 5, 1993, pp. 54–63), argued against incentive systems, writing that:

> Research suggests that, by and large, rewards succeed at securing one thing only: temporary compliance. When it comes to producing lasting change in attitudes and behavior, however, rewards, like punishment, are strikingly ineffective. Once the rewards run out, people revert to their old behaviors. Studies show that offering incentives for losing weight, quitting smoking, using seat belts, or (in the case of children) acting generously is not only less effective than other strategies but often proves worse than doing nothing at all. Incentives, a version of what psychologists call extrinsic motivators, do not alter the attitudes that underlie our behaviors. They do not create an enduring commitment to any value or action. Rather, incentives merely and temporarily change what we do.

Key to the long-term success of these plans is the understanding that quality cannot be compromised in the quest for greater productivity.

Pilot programs of profit-sharing may be tried in one locale to determine the worker reaction to these incentives. If the program works, company-wide implementation should be undertaken or some resentment may come from those employees not receiving profit-sharing. The operations manager is concerned with efficient production and high quality and must find the means to gain the employee commitment to achieve operational goals. The manager can only do this if there is a feeling that the pay system is fair.

MOTIVATION

For many years, researchers have grappled with the question, "What motivates workers?" In 1959, Frederick Herzberg studied 200 engineers and accountants and asked them about times they felt especially good and times they felt especially bad on their jobs. He concluded that there were two main factors involved in motivation. *Maintenance factors* must be present in a job or their absence results in dissatisfaction. These factors are:

1. Company policy and administration.
2. Technical supervision.
3. Interpersonal relations with supervisor.
4. Interpersonal relations with peers.
5. Interpersonal relations with subordinates.
6. Salary.
7. Job security.
8. Personal life.
9. Work conditions.
10. Status.

Motivational factors can lead to job satisfaction if they are present. Their absence does not lead to job dissatisfaction. These factors are:

1. Achievement.
2. Recognition.
3. Advancement.
4. The work itself.
5. The possibility of personal growth.
6. Responsibility.

Herzberg's most interesting finding was that money was a maintenance factor and not a motivating factor. There has been some controversy surrounding Herzberg's theory. Some critics argued that the results could not be generalized beyond accountants and engineers. However, 35 years after Herzberg's studies, his research is still considered important to the understanding of motivation.

Intuitively, we know that different things motivate different people, and it is the art of management to discover what those things are and parcel them out equitably. Further, motivating factors may vary according to culture and national origin. Operations managers must find ways to keep their workers motivated when increased compensation is out of the question.

IMPROVING THE QUALITY OF WORK LIFE

What is a high quality of work life? The answer, of course, will differ from person to person, but a starting point is the physical environment in which work is performed. The workplace should be clean, noise should be minimized, and all efforts should be made to create a pleasant surrounding. We often hear of writers and artists who draw inspiration from a certain place that they love. It may not be possible to build a babbling brook around an assembly line, but more thought should go into the interior design of a plant or headquarters than is presently done.

When workers look forward to going to work, then they have a high quality of work life. This may simply be due to the fact that they like their fellow workers and look forward to their daily interactions with them. It could also mean that managers have established a good environment for enjoyable work.

The quality of life in the city or town of company location has much to do with the employees' attitude about work. The many hours some people spend commuting to and from work takes away from personal lives and increases stress levels. Many firms are locating away from large metropolitan centers to reduce stress on their work force.

Recruitment and Selection

Operations managers need a good working relationship with the human resource managers who are responsible for recruiting and selecting new employees. The operations manager's role in this process differs from firm to firm, but it is essential that the human resources and operations departments communicate each other's needs and requirements.

Key questions to answer in recruitment and selection:

1. What is the prospect's attitude toward work?
2. Do the prospect's outside interests mesh with current employees?
3. Is the prospect willing to relocate if necessary?
4. What are the prospect's financial expectations?

5. What work experiences can the prospect bring to the job?
6. How often has the prospect changed jobs in the past?
7. Does the prospect come with good recommendations?
8. What skills, knowledge, and prior training does the prospect possess?
9. Does the prospect appear friendly and personable and able to work with others?
10. What are the prospect's prior accomplishments?

Operations managers need to thoroughly evaluate prospective employees. Some human resource departments administer a bevy of tests to determine the personality and psychological makeup of the applicant. A background check is an absolute essential task, verifying the education and past employment record of the new employee. Ignoring this step can have dire consequences.

Labor Relations

A good labor/management relationship is characterized by an attitude of partnership. Some labor unions perpetuate a "them-versus-us" theme, creating an often needless adversarial relationship. Communication between management and labor is key to fostering a true partnership. Truthful presentation of the financial status of the firm and managerial goals and directions, all need to be communicated.

Performance Evaluation

Employees want to know how they are doing. In most companies, an annual performance evaluation is conducted between supervisor and worker, and the worker is then told of his or her shortcomings and accomplishments. The most important aspect of a performance evaluation is attitude. If the employee looks forward to the evaluation with dread, something is wrong with the process. This should be a motivational time, not a punitive session. The supervisor should review the goals of the prior period and how well the employee did with respect to those goals. Areas of needed improvement should be noted, but so should areas of accomplishment and personal development.

Conducting performance evaluations is an important part of a manager's job, but one in which most managers have little or no preparation. The evaluation process can be mishandled by a manager, so that the worker feels that their shortcomings are all they are told about, and a negative feeling is communicated that adversely effects the work atmosphere.

Some evaluation systems result in a total score for performance. For example, a staff of clerks may be evaluated on ten performance criterion with a 5–point scale. The optimum total score might be 50 points. Since the evaluations are quite subjective, it is important to tie the employee score to the average rating administered by the rater. One supervisor may feel a 3 score on a 5–point scale represents good performance and another may believe 4 is a good score. It would be unfair to all the employees scored by the former supervisor to compare them with employees scored by the latter supervisor. Raters should receive training to avoid common evaluation mistakes such as the halo effect, reverse halo effect, recency effect, and past record anchoring.

Leap and Crino (1989) proposed a five step process in developing a performance appraisal system:

1. Review equal employment opportunity legal requirements.
2. Determine the uses for the appraisal information.
3. Establish the evaluation system. Design and implement the system.
4. Examine the appraisal data and fair employment requirements.
5. Use the appraisal data for appropriate purposes.

The selected performance criterion should work toward the accomplishment of the organizational mission. Similar to the selection of productivity measurements, some criteria are inappropriate and can cause counterproductive behaviors.

The problems with performance evaluation are in the actual execution of the evaluation. The evaluation must be taken seriously, and some managers disavow their responsibility immediately with comments like, "Let's get this over with!" Employees should not approach their evaluation as if they are going to the dentist. Regular feedback on employee performance takes much of the mystery out of the evaluation. It is not fair to tell an employee 364 days a year, "Great job! great going!" and then write a poor evaluation. In cases where performance could stand improvement, the manager should not wait for the evaluation date to discuss the matter.

Women in Operations Work Roles

An important human resources issue for operations managers concerns the changing roles of women in the workplace. The sexual "liberation" of the 1970s gave way to the sexual "harassment" of the 1980s as men and women struggled to define appropriate workplace behavior. Economic and social forces have changed so that women are *in* the workforce and men will eventually grow comfortable in working with and for them. Although women have made inroads in many service operations positions, they are still minor forces in manufacturing. But many traditionally male work roles are now accepting women, including construction, assembly line work, transportation, and the legal and medical professions.

There are two basic models that explain women's role in management: the equity model and the complementary contribution model (Adler and Izraeli, 1988). The equity model assumes that men and women are equally capable of contributing to organizations. Female managers are expected to think and act similar to their male counterparts who hold similar positions. Effectiveness is measured against male norms. This model is most pervasive in U.S. companies. The complementary contribution model is based on assumed gender differences. Women are capable of making different, but equally valuable, contributions to the organization than men. This model is most often seen in France and other European countries. The usefulness of each model should be evaluated under a cultural context and historical background. The question is not whether one model is better than another. Rather, the question is: should similarity be emphasized? To what extent should differences be viewed as potential resources? To what extent should uniqueness be viewed as an asset rather than a constraint? Table 7–1 provides a comparison between these two models.

Although there are only a handful of women CEOs in U.S. corporations, it is only a matter of time before women assume the leadership of major corporations in the United States. Other countries, notably Japan, have been slower to promote women into managerial positions. Table 7–2 provides a comparison between working women of Japan and the United States.

One consulting firm has offered the following observations that help explain an underrepresentation of women in managerial and professional positions (Tan, 1984). Companies are reluctant to hire a woman to head a department staffed by men; companies hesitate to employ women to supervise plants, shipyards, or construction sites that are traditionally considered as male domains; employers often doubt whether women (especially working mothers) will take their careers seriously and be willing to work the long hours necessary to be successful. Unfavorable social norms such as the expectation of women to play different roles in different circumstances and organizational structures that prevent women from advancement.

Managers working in their nonnative environments must face not only an unfamiliar work environment, but must cope with a foreign language and different cultural norms and standards. The cultural constraints in some countries particularly pose a greater challenge to female expatriate managers. One female expatriate to Japan said, "Although I was the best qualified, I was not offered the position in Japan

Table 7–1

Women's Role in Management

Assumptions	Equity model	Complementary contribution
Fundamental assumptions	similarity	difference
Men and women's contribution	identical	complementary
Fairness based on	equity	valuing difference
Strategic goal	equal access	recognizing and valuing differences
Assessment	quantitative	qualitative
Measured by	statistical proportion of women at each hierarchical level	assessing women's contribution to organizational goals
Process	counting women	assessing women's contribution
Measurement of effectiveness		
Women's contribution	identical to men's	complementary to men's
Norms	identical for men and women	unique to men and women
Based on	historical "male" norms	women's own contribution
Referent	men	women
Acculturation process	assimilation	synergy
Expected behavior	standardized	differentiated
Based on	male norms	female norms
Essence	"dress for success" business suit	feminine attire
Example	United States: "The melting pot"	France "Vive la difference!"

(Source: Adler and Izraeli, 1988, p. 4)

Table 7–2
Women in the Work Place: Japan Versus U.S.

	Japan	U.S.
Percent of all women who work	50.7%	57.8
Percent of working women who work part time	30.7	25.4
Percent women earn compared with men	57.1	70.0
Percent of women in these jobs: Attorneys	9.0	21.4
Doctors	11.0	20.4
Management	8.8	47.3
CPAs	2.9	51.2
Farming, fishing	29.3	15.0
Manual labor	27.2	19.0
CEOs of top companies	0.0	1.0
Members of Diet/Congress	6.8	10.0

(Source: Gannett News Service)

until the senior Japanese manager in Tokyo said, 'We are very flexible in Japan.' Then they sent me" (Adler, 1988, p. 238). The cultural tradition in each country defines social norms and informal rules that in turn, help shape people's way of thinking and frame of references. For instance, a well-known Confucian saying states that a woman should obey her father as daughter, her husband as wife, and her son as mother. Although the anti-Confucian movement in 1970s was supposed to create a more favorable environment for women in China, women in management positions are underrepresented, and their pay is inferior to their male counterparts. Some Asians seldom encounter a female supervisor and may doubt the competence of one they encounter. One female expatriate to the People's Republic of China said, "I speak Chinese, which is a plus. But they'd talk to the men, not to me. They'd assume that I, as a woman, had no authority. The Chinese want to deal with top-level people, and there is always a man at a higher level" (Adler, 1988, p. 243).

While some female expatriate North American managers cited a number of disadvantages in being female, most female expatriates reported such professional advantages to being female as high visibility, accessibility, and memorability. In Adler's study (1988), one female expatriate to Thailand related that being a woman was not a detriment. Another female expatriate to Japan said, "Women are better at putting people at ease. The traditional woman's role . . . inspires confidence and trust. They assumed I must be good if I was sent." (p. 241)

Gender issues are more pertinent to successful operations management as more and more women are entering a well-established male preserve and tapping into traditionally male-held operations management positions. Increasingly, women are to be found on the assembly line, in construction, in garages, and many other non-traditional gender roles. Increasingly, more women managers are sent abroad to manage international operations. No matter whether it is a domestic operation or an international operation and no matter whether we are managing female employees in a foreign country or dealing with foreign clients' and colleagues' initial expectations of female expatriate managers, it is imperative that gender differences don't become problematical and impede performance.

OPERATIONS AND THE ENVIRONMENT

Another growing issue for operations managers is the interaction with the environment. Perhaps no one business function has more to do with the environment than operations. Operations managers must strictly obey local environmental regulations and are sometimes found in the ethical dilemma of being asked by their employer to find ways to compromise those regulations. In such difficult situations, managers often opt to keep their jobs rather than obey the law. This is the sort of logic that has led to many business disasters. The question of whether an issue is right for the employee or for society boils down to personal ethics, ultimately, and hopefully operations managers are on the right side. Some issues are particularly thorny, such as the issue of jobs versus development. This becomes an almost personal decision of whether your job is more important than society and nature.

SUMMARY

Many managers thrive on the technical aspects of operations: the excitement of laying out a new plant, the selection of innovative new forms of automation, and managing inventory. In some cases, this is what draws them into a career in production. To achieve success, however, there is no way around the fact that a manager must know how to direct people. Those who are incompetent with people are best relegated to staff positions where they can deal with technology.

Managers of the 1990s must have people *and* technology skills. How does a manager learn how to direct others? Where do they learn how to recruit and select good workers? Where do they receive training in personnel evaluation and review?

Employees who receive either undergraduate or graduate training in management have learned the fundamentals. In tennis terms, they know how to serve and volley, and they know the rules of the game.

But receiving lessons in tennis does not prepare a player to return a serve from Martina Navratilova or Boris Becker. The fundamentals teach the basics of the game, and then the player plays against real competition. When college graduates are faced with managing real employees, they may forget all of their fundamentals at first and then return to them after a series of managerial mistakes. All great managers make mistakes while they are developing, and sometimes make bigger mistakes when they have supposedly matured. The point is that these lessons are best learned through direct experience. New employees who come to a firm without the basic managerial fundamentals must receive management development training at some point, unless they are designated for staff work.

The successful operations manager knows the value of people in accomplishing the firm's mission, and the people, if motivated, will help achieve that mission.

REFERENCES

Adler, N. J. (1988). "Pacific Basin Managers: A Gaijin, Not a Woman." in N. J. Adler and D. N. Izraeli (eds). *Women in Management Worldwide*. New York: M. E. Sharpe Inc., pp. 226–249.

Adler, N. J. and D. N. Izraeli (1988). "Women in Management Worldwide," in N. J. Adler and D. N. Izraeli (eds). *Women in Management Worldwide*. New York: M.E. Sharpe Inc. pp. 3–16.

Cherrington, David J. (1991). *The Management of Human Resources*. Boston: Allyn & Bacon.

Hayes, R., S. Wheelwright, and K. Clark (1988). *Dynamic Manufacturing*. New York: The Free Press.

Herzberg, F., B. Mausner, and B. Snyderman (1959). *The Motivation to Work*, (2nd ed.). New York: Wiley.

Kohn, A. (1993). "Why Incentive Plans Cannot Work." *Harvard Business Review*, 71(5):54–63.

Leap, T. L. and M. D. Crino (1989). *Personnel/Human Resource Management*. New York: Macmillan.

Tan, A. "Women Urged to Take High-Tech Road." *The Straits Times*, November, 1984, p. 19.

8

Cultural Impact on Global Operations

As the conventional barriers of countries, regions, and states become less meaningful, global businesses and cultural networks are increasingly shaping the world economy. In this chapter, we discuss why it is important to consider cultural factors in the context of global operations management, what defines culture, and how to manage issues of cultural diversity.

WHY CULTURE MATTERS

EuroDisney, the world's largest theme park, was greeted with intense resistance even before its opening in France. Critics said that EuroDisney was too American, and not European. The French were reluctant to embrace the American popular culture. Under such a cloud of skepticism, EuroDisney has proved to be a financial disappointment. Tokyo Disney, on the other hand, met a quite different reception. The Japanese were eager to accept the Americanized theme park and were fascinated by American culture. The attractions are almost identical to those in America. Of course, there are alterations and additions that adapt to Japanese taste, such as Japanese-style restaurants. The early enthusiasm and careful planning have been rewarded with the financial success of Tokyo Disney.

These two examples illustrate how cultural differences can impact the success or failure of global operations. Whether a firm is involved in a joint venture or building a subsidiary in another country or simply buying materials from another country, there is always the need to interact with business partners, suppliers, and employees from different cultures. Value, attitudes, customs, ritual, and other cultural elements can all have significant impact on the interaction. Understanding cultural differences may considerably smooth the making of business deals by reducing unnecessary cultural barriers.

Operations management deals with converting inputs (raw materials, capital, people, and management skills) to outputs (desirable goods and services). Global operations involves planning, organizing, and managing people, resources, technology, and processes to make this conversion effective and efficient on a global scale. Cultural differences can impact on interactions among operations managers and employees from different cultural backgrounds, on how resources are used, on how technologies are transferred across borders, and on how process improvements are achieved. For instance, Japanese workers are more accustomed to the participative management style. Authoritative management style may make them uncomfortable and prove ultimately unproductive. People in some areas view certain forests and mountains as embodying special spiritual meanings, and therefore, unplanned and excessive tapping of resources in those regions may be regarded as a lack of respect for the local culture.

When in Rome, do as the Romans do. This rule is applicable for global operations. The cultural traditions in each country define the ground rules governing the behavior of the local inhabitants. Cultural illiteracy and incompetency often lead to the loss of a lot of money resulting from breaches of contract, loss of sales, customer alienation, and other sorts of business failures.

Before we can learn to manage issues that have to do with cultural diversity, we first need to know what constitutes a culture.

WHAT IS CULTURE?

If personality determines a person's identity, then culture defines the identity of a human group. James Fallows (1989) refers to the way that ordinary people voluntarily behave as "culture." Czinkpta and his colleagues (1992) define culture as an integrated system of learned behavior patterns that are characteristics of the members of any given society. After analyzing more than 160 definitions of culture, Kroeber and Kluckhohn (1985) offer one of the most comprehensive definitions of culture:

> Culture consists of patterns, explicit and implicit, of and for behavior acquired and transmitted by symbols, constituting the distinctive achievement of human groups, including their embodiment in their artifacts; the essential core of culture consists of traditional (i.e., historically derived and selected) ideas and especially their attached values; culture systems may,

on the one hand, be considered as products of action, on the other, as conditioning elements of future action (p.11).

Therefore, culture has the following characteristics:

1. it is shared by members of the society;
2. it is learned and transmitted from one generation to the next; and
3. it shapes behavior and the way of thinking.

Hofstede (1980) viewed culture as the collective programming of the mind that distinguishes the members of one human group from another. There are subcultures within a culture. For instance, there is an Hispanic subculture within the American culture. Subcultures are usually shared by a group of people of similar education level, socioeconomic status, gender, religion, race, age group, or ethnic background. Some countries are more homogeneous than others. The cultures of Japan and Saudi Arabia are considered more homogeneous, whereas the American culture can be viewed as more heterogeneous. It is also quite common to distinguish between cross-culture and intraculture.

CULTURAL DIMENSIONS

Culture is multidimensional. Some researchers have attempted to define dimensions on which culture can be meaningfully ordered. It is Hofstede (1980) whose dimensions of culture are the most comprehensive and widely quoted.

On the basis of international attitudes survey of 66 countries, Hofstede was able to define four dimensions of culture in power distance, uncertainty avoidance, individualism, and masculinity. The following discussion of these four dimensions is largely based on the results of his study presented in his book *Culture's Consequences* (1980).

The first dimension is *power distance*. It measures the interpersonal power between the supervisor and the subordinate. The power distance index (PDI) is derived from the questions that measure perceptions of the supervisor's style of decision making, perceptions of colleagues' fear to disagree with supervisors, and the type of decision-making style that subordinates prefer in their supervisor.

High PDI countries such as the Philippines, Mexico, Venezuela, and India present the following major characteristics: Parents put high value on their children's obedience; conformity is highly valued; employees are reluctant to disagree with their supervisor; managers are more satisfied with directive or persuasive superior; and managers' decision-making styles are perceived to be more autocratic and paternalistic. Low PDI countries such as Austria, Israel, and Denmark exhibit the following major traits: Independence is highly valued; employees are less afraid of disagreeing with their superior; close supervision is negatively evaluated by employees; managers are more satisfied with a participative superior; and managers are perceived to make decisions after consulting with subordinates.

One of the main implications of the power distance dimension in organizations is organizational structure. Organizations in a high PDI culture are likely to give rise to greater centralization and taller organization pyramids, whereas those in a low PDI culture tend to have less centralization and flatter organization structures.

Uncertainty avoidance originates from the fact that the tolerance for uncertainty varies considerably among people in subsidiaries in different countries. Three indicators of rule orientation, employment stability, and stress are used to produce this index (UAI).

Countries such as Greece, Portugal, Belgium, and Japan score high in this dimension. Those countries are usually characterized as having higher anxiety levels in population, higher job stress, more emotional resistance to change, greater generation gap, fear of failure, fewer people prepared to live abroad, lower ambition for individual advancement, tendency to stay with the same employer, more worry about the future, being less risk-taking, and suspicious towards foreigners as managers. Cultures such as those of Singapore, Denmark, Sweden, and Hong Kong score low in this dimension. They usually exhibit such traits as having lower anxiety level in population, less emotional resistance to change, smaller generation gap, hope of success, acceptance of foreigners as managers, large fraction of people prepared to live abroad, stronger ambition for individual advancement, less hesitation to change employers, greater readiness to live by the day, and being more risk-taking.

Consequences of national uncertainty avoidance index differences are likely to determine organizational structures and processes. A great need for uncertainty avoidance leads to more structuring of activities, more written rules, lower labor turnover, less ambitious employees, higher satisfaction scores, and more ritual behavior. Managers are less willing to making individual and risky decisions and are more involved in details.

Individualism describes the relationship between the individual and the collectivity of a given society. Individualism is seen as a source of creativity and well-being and, as a consequence, a proud trait for American culture, whereas collectivism is accentuated over individualism in most Asian countries. The individualism index (IDV) is mainly composed of six work goals (personal time, freedom, challenge, use of skills, physical conditions, and training). For instance, the IDV is strongly correlated with personal time phrased as having a job that leaves you sufficient time for personal or family life.

Countries such as the United States, Australia, Great Britain, and Canada are usually classified as high IDV countries. Importance of the employees' personal life and emotional independence from the company are emphasized. Individual initiative is socially encouraged. Individual decisions are considered better than group decisions. Managers consider having autonomy more important and aspire to leadership. Countries such as Peru, Pakistan, Colombia, and Venezuela are more collective-oriented. Employees show more emotional dependence on the company. Individual initiative is less socially encouraged. Group decisions are considered better than individual decisions. Managers consider having job security more important and aspire to conformity.

The level of individualism will affect the level of employees' willingness to comply with organizational requirements. In high IDV countries, employees are expected to look after their own interests, since lifelong employment is not likely to be offered. Organizational policies and practices should allow for and promote individual initiative, and management should endorse modern management ideas.

The fourth dimension is called *masculinity*, with femininity as its opposite pole. Advancements and earnings seem more important to men, whereas friendly atmosphere and position security seem more pertinent for women. Hofstede employs the term masculinity to describe the dominant force of the society as that of male alertness or female nurturing. The masculinity index (MAS) is measured on work goal scores. The goals include manager, cooperation, desirable area, employment security, challenge, advancement, recognition, and earnings.

Japan ranks the highest in terms of MAS. German-speaking countries (Austria, Switzerland, and Germany) also tend to score high on this dimension. High MAS countries are usually portrayed as having stronger achievement motivation, greater work centrality, greater social role attributed to corporation, higher job stress, greater value difference between men and women in the same jobs, and aspiration to recognition. The company's interference in private life is generally accepted and people prefer more salary to shorter working hours. At the lowest end of the masculinity dimension are Finland, Denmark, Norway, Sweden, and the Netherlands. Low MAS countries are usually described as having weaker achievement motivation, work is less central in people's lives, there is a greater social role attributed to institutions other than corporations, lower job stress, smaller to no value difference between men and women in the same jobs, and less interest in recognition. The company's interference in private life is rejected, and people prefer shorter working hours to more salary.

The effect of the masculinity dimension on organizations can be seen on the issue of job restructuring. In a masculine culture, opportunities for recognition, advancement, and challenge is given particular import-ance, whereas in a feminine culture, cooperation and the working atmosphere are underscored.

These dimensions are not separate. They are interacting with each other to define and impact culture. For instance, countries scoring higher in power distance tend to have low individualism and countries with small power distance tend to have high individualism. There are some exceptions, such as Spain, France, and Italy, which exhibit both large power distance and high individualism. Anglo and Scan-dinavian countries have small power distance and weak uncertainty avoidance; Southeast Asian countries exhibit large power distance and weak uncertainty avoidance; German-speaking countries demonstrate small power distance and strong uncertainty avoidance; and Latin countries display large power distance and strong uncer-tainty avoidance.

CULTURAL ELEMENTS

The culture of a society usually is reflected in the values, attitudes, and behavior demonstrated by group members. Individual members of a society express their cultural orientation through the values they hold about life and the world. These values shape their attitudes towards a certain event or object. Religion, tradition, customs, lan-guage, and nonverbal language are all considered important elements of what we call culture. In this section, we will broadly talk about (1) values; (2) religion, tradition, and customs; (3) language; and (4) nonverbal language. We will also briefly discuss other noncultural factors that can have a significant bearing on globalizing operations.

Values and Attitudes

According to Kluckhohn (1951), "a value is a conception, explicit or implicit, distinctive of an individual or characteristic of a group, of the desirable which influences the selection from available means and ends of actions" (p. 395). Values are relatively general beliefs that define what is right and wrong and specify the priorities of the society. What is considered a right business practice in one culture may be viewed as unacceptable in another culture on the basis of a different value sys-tems. Misunderstanding often occurs when people use their own value systems to frame their opinions or make judgments about events without considering the appropriate cultural background against which such events arise. Values direct people of a society to attend to certain goals and subordinate others. When your foreign business partner is not as attentive and as responsive as you would expect to the proposal or suggestion you make, instead of jumping to the conclusion that your idea is not respected or favorable, it is worthwhile finding out whether they have different priorities. Maybe they have other goals that are considered more important and need immediate attention before they can evaluate your idea.

Myrdal (1971) pointed out that values are related to economic development. In Asia, certain religiously sanctioned beliefs can act as obstacles among people to getting new ideas and plans accepted and as resistance to making changes. He found that the following values and ideals are necessary to facilitate economic performance in some of the Asian regions: efficiency, diligence, orderliness, punctuality, frugality, scrupulous honesty, rationality in decision-making, preparedness for change, alertness to opportunities as they arise in a changing world, energetic enterprise, integrity and self-reliance, cooperativeness, and willingness to take the long view.

Value toward work, wealth, achievement, change, risk perception, and scientific discovery can all have an important impact on economic development. Certain values can also influence organizational behavior, corporate culture, motivation and reward system, interpersonal relationship, group behavior, communication, and conflict resolution (Adler, 1991). For instance, most Americans believe in individual achievement and, as such, their reward system is more geared toward individual merits. China has always been a collectivistic society and emphasizes the maintenance of good relationships among people. The resulting reward system stresses equality among its societal members and is often less incentive compatible than those found in Western countries.

Attitudes reflect the opinions that an individual holds toward events, acts, objects, or persons. They are much influenced by the value system that an individual adheres to. Because of the strong influence of Confucianism in China, modesty is instilled among its people and considered a highly desirable and essential quality for achieving any kind of goal. This explains why a Chinese, when praised for speaking fluent English, tends to reply "No, I don't speak English very well" instead of "thank you." The way people react to outside events are often molded by the attitudes they inherit from their unique national experience. For instance, the prevalent optimism about science and technology in most developed countries probably derives from the prominent role that technological innovations have played in those societies since the Industrial Revolution.

Religion, Tradition, and Customs

Religion is "a socially shared set of beliefs, ideas, and actions that relate to a reality that cannot be verified empirically yet is believed to affect the course of natural and human events" (Terstra and David, 1991, p. 73). Such a belief can affect a person's behavior and action.

A classification by the World Christian Encyclopedia provides the following partition of religions: literate religions, nonliterate religions, and nonreligious and atheist groups. Nonliterate religions encompass Chinese folk religion, tribalist, and shamanist beliefs. An incomplete list of literate religions include Buddhism, Christianity, Hinduism, Judaism, Islam, and others (including Sikh, Confucian, Shinto, Baha'i, and Parsi). Among these, Buddhism, Christianity, Hinduism, Islam, and nonliterate religions are considered major religion groups since, taken together, their followers represent about three quarters of the world's population.

Religion can impact international operations, especially in a country where it is part of the mainstream culture. The fact that religious factors can be an important source of political risk is witnessed by the numerous political instabilities attributable to religious conflicts around the globe. In general, political instability is more likely to occur in countries that have several major religions, that are diverse in their racial and ethnic makeup, and that have a history of internal conflicts.

Religion is often closely tied to regional economic performance. The North Atlantic Protestant polities are considered the most affluent regions (Terpstra and David, 1991, p. 98). Resource endowments are clearly illustrated in Islamic polities, OPEC or non-OPEC. To globalize operations, it is necessary to understand how religion can fit in to economic development, how religion may support or interfere with the corporate culture, and how religion may impact the specific business conduct and practices of international operations.

Religion can have a direct impact on production and operations management. Each region has certain calendar days that entail specific spiritual meanings. Operations managers need to be aware of these religious events in the host country and schedule their operations accordingly. Scheduling production during the Hindu Tai Ponkal festival is just like asking Americans to work during Christmas. When the delivery date coincides with a major holiday, for example, the operations manager is advised to schedule the production so that it is finished before the holiday. Lack of this knowledge may cause missing the delivery date and risk alienating the local employees if they are forced to work on such occasions. Another example illustrates how religious considerations can affect the choice of location. One advertising agency decided to open a branch in Thailand. They rented an office. However, a Buddhist statue was right across the street below the office level. The manager was warned that it would never succeed. After a year, the business was struggling. The manager moved to a new location and business started to boom. Why would the old location not work? "You never put yourself above Buddha."

Religion can also influence consumer demand patterns and choices. The sales of food items rise during the Muslim Ramadan festival. A knowledgeable manager can make use of this information and increase production before the festival and inventory enough for the occasion. Practicing Muslims do not eat pork, and therefore, restaurants that feature pork dishes cannot expect to sell well in Islamic countries.

Religion is but one aspect of the local environment that also includes other local traditions, mannerisms, and customs. The smooth execution and the ultimate success of any international operations require that its managers understand, and immerse themselves in, the traditions and customs of the local culture. Take the example of women's social status, which varies across different societal structures. According to Japanese tradition, women are expected to withdraw from employment upon marriage, even if quite successful. This is clearly a social norm whose impact on managerial assignment policies cannot be ignored.

In business negotiations, a delegate from America may expect to start serious discussions in the interest of reaching a deal as soon as possible. However, settling a seemingly simple issue may take their foreign partners several days when other issues are mixed in. Sometimes, this is due to the desire of the foreign negotiators to get to know their counterparts personally before they are ready to embark on the "real business" on the agenda. As is often the case, building a trusting, long-lasting relationship is deemed more important than merely making a quick deal. If these subtle differences go unappreciated, a Western negotiator tends to get frustrated with their foreign partners' "inaction and inefficiency." Precisely due to the use of different frames of reference in business dealings, some Asian businessmen accuse their American partners of being too pushy or even insincere. Cooperation among business people from different cultural backgrounds has a better chance to materialize and flourish if such misunderstandings are avoided.

Learning about the local rituals and mannerisms is not as difficult as it may sound. If one is invited to a Japanese house for a tea ceremony and the hosts take off their shoes before entering the room, it is safe to assume that it is proper to follow their lead. Obviously, not all foreign customs are as observable. When giving a gift to a Japanese friend, for instance, one should avoid giving four of anything because the number "four" in Japanese is pronounced the same way as "death." Unintentional mistakes are most likely to occur when a manager has yet to learn the local ways of life. Fortunately, there are ways to avoid blunders and minimize unnecessary mistakes: taking classes on the traditions and customs of the destination country before going abroad, reading books on that country, asking friends who have been there to share their anecdotes and experiences, learning the basics of that country's history and language, and being observant and ready to ask for advice from the local people.

Language

Language is the most recognizable component of culture. It not only conveys information but also helps define socialization through understanding, classifying, coding, prioritizing, and justifying reality. Multiplicity of languages and cultural diversity represent both a constraint and a benefit to globalizing operations. For operations managers who are bilingual or multilingual and have a strong desire to learn new languages and about other cultures, language capability can be an advantage in business dealings.

Language capability serves four distinct roles in international business (Ricks, 1983). First, language is important in gathering information and evaluating market conditions. Managers can personally talk to the local people and employees without relying on the opinions of others. People are usually more comfortable conversing in their own language. Communicating with people in their native language enables the managers to get first-hand information. Second, language also helps the managers to gain access to and even participate in the different phases of the local societal development. Being able to communicate in the local language often makes a favorable impression on the local people and this can make a big difference. Third, language capability is important in communications inside of the company as well. The firms must be able to communicate with customers, suppliers, and the host government. Expatriate managers must communicate with indigenous managers and employees who may not be able to speak languages other than the native language. If the operations managers are not conversant in the local language, they would have to rely on an interpreter in company meetings. Fourth, in some cultures, most of the information is explicitly contained in the word. In other cultures, it is more important to understand and listen to what have been implied than what is actually said. A reply of "yes" could mean "no," given the context.

There are over 4,000 languages spoken in the world today. This figure does not include many dialects a language can have. India alone has an estimated 3,000 dialects. Over 20 countries have more than one official language. Singapore, Belgium, and Switzerland each has four official languages. On the basis of population alone, Chinese is the most spoken language in the world. English, French, and Spanish have spread throughout Africa and the Americas since the era of colonialism. Russia's dominance over Eastern Europe has led to a growing use of Russian. English is perhaps the most popular language in the business world. It serves as an official language for many countries.

Our thinking is largely limited by the categories and availability of words. Each language reflects a particular world view and the reflection of the universe may change from one tongue to another. For instance, there are over 6,000 different words for camel, its parts, and equipments associated with it in Arabic. The Eskimos have more words to describe snow than most other languages. English is relatively rich in its vocabulary depicting computer-related technology.

When American managers are communicating to their business partners or employees who speak English, they should be aware of the regional differences in its usages such as pronunciation, slang, and colloquial expressions. As George Bernard Shaw once said, "England and America are divided by a common language." Terms such as flat, torch, and petrol used in Britain are called apartment, flashlight, and gas respectively by the Americans. A Scottish accent may sound rather foreign to most Americans just as Texan English would to the Australians.

Managers may want to know what percentage of the local people speak a certain language, at what occasions it is spoken, and what other dialectical variations exist. In Hong Kong, for instance, English is more likely to be used in formal meetings and business dealings. During lunch conversations, however, foreign managers may be appreciated and well liked if they speak Cantonese.

If operations managers cannot speak the local language and have to rely on an interpreter, they should be aware of some of the potential problems that are likely to occur. First is that there could be no precise equivalent of a concept in another language. It is often the case that direct translation may not be the most faithful translation. Second is that the different shades of meaning may be overlooked by the interpreter, and therefore, subtlety can easily become lost. Third is that, due to various reasons, words and meanings could be completely twisted, blunted, or lost in the translation process. Braniff Airlines' "Fly in Leather" was translated as "Fly Naked" for the company's Latin American campaign (Czinkota et al. 1992). Coca-Cola is translated into "drink it and feel happy" in Chinese. It is a much better translation that conveys the appeal of the product. The translation process can be the source of many errors. However, errors can be reduced by a careful selection of translators and the use of back-translation method.

Some Air France employees collected a number of poor attempts at English that are quite unintentionally humorous. (Axtell, 1993).

In a Tokyo hotel:
Is forbidden to steal hotel towels please. If you are not a person to do such thing is please not to read notis.

In a Belgrade hotel elevator:
To move the cabin, push button for wishing floor. If the cabin should enter more persons, each one should press a number of wishing floor. Driving is then going alphabetically by national order.

In a Paris hotel elevator:
Please leave your values at the front desk.

In a hotel in Athens:
Visitors are expected to complain at the office between the hours of 9 and 11 A.M. daily.

In a Yugoslavian hotel:
The flattening of underwear with pleasure is the job of the chambermaid.

In a Japanese hotel:
You are invited to take advantage of the chambermaid.

On the menu of a Swiss restaurant:
Our wines leave you nothing to hope for.

In a Bangkok dry cleaner:
Drop your trousers here for best results.

In a Rhodes tailor shop:
Order your summer suit. Because if big rush we will execute customers in strict rotation.

In a Zurich hotel:
Because of the impropriety of entertaining guests of the opposite sex in the bedroom, it is suggested that the lobby be used for this purpose.

In an advertisement by a Hong Kong dentist:
Teeth extracted by the latest Methodists.

In a Rome laundry:
Ladies, leave your clothes here and spend the afternoon having a good time.

Advertisement for donkey rides in Thailand:
Would you like to ride on your own ass?

In a Bangkok temple:
It is forbidden to enter a woman, even a foreigner if dressed as a man.

In a Tokyo bar:
Special cocktails for the ladies with nuts.

On the door of a Moscow hotel room:
If this is your first visit to Russia, you are welcome to it.

In a Norwegian cocktail lounge:
Ladies are requested not to have children in the bar.

In the office of a Roman doctor:
Specialist in women and other diseases.

In an Acapulco hotel:
The manager has personally passed all the water served here.

Although these mistakes are more funny than offensive, language mistakes can offend people unintentionally or cause other communication problems. The moral to the story is: be prepared. Study the language before arriving, and get constant tutoring. Make sure important business negotiations are staffed with skilled interpreters when more than one language is used.

Nonverbal Language

Managers not only have to understand and listen to what is said but also try to understand and familiarize themselves with the hidden language of the local culture In some Western cultures, time is viewed as a linear construct that consists of a continuum of past, present, and future. Time is almost equated with money in that it can be saved or wasted. Punctuality is appreciated in the business world and often interpreted as being efficient and showing respect for others. In some Spanish-speaking cultures, American businessmen are often frustrated with and irritated by their local partners' lack of punctuality. However, most people in those countries do not have the same notion of linearity of time. They perceive time as a circular system without making a clear distinction among a past, present, and future. Time is not equated with money. Being late is often seen as the person being important and having a lot of businesses to attend to.

Sometimes managers may run into communication problems even though they speak the local language perfectly. Incorrect body language can also lead to erroneous interpretation and unintentionally cause offense to the other party. For instance, direct eye contact is less common in Japan than in Western countries. What is considered as an honest look in the eye in a Western country could be taken as a sign of disrespect or personal confrontation in another.

Even unintentional and unconscious gestures could cause discomfort to someone from a different culture. In some cultures, hugging is as common as handshaking. For someone who does not share this cultural background and has an aversion to such body contacts, hugging may cause great discomfort.

Facial expression, hand gesture, body signs, and other nonverbal expressions all convey a certain meaning based on the individual culture. Even the most popular hand sign V, which signifies "victory" to most European countries, means two of something, such as two more beers, in non-British–oriented countries.

Axtell (1993) has listed some of the popular international gestures. Here are a few examples from his listing (p.45):

Eyebrow Raised: In Tonga, it means "yes" or "I agree." In Peru, it means "money" or "pay me."

Chin Flick: In Italy, it means "not interested" or "buzz off." In Brazil and Paraguay, it means "I don't know."

Blink: In Taiwan, blinking the eye at someone is considered impolite.

Fingers Circled: It is widely accepted as okay sign by Americans. In Brazil and Germany, it is considered vulgar or obscene. It is regarded as impolite in Greece and Russia. It means "money" to Japanese people and "zero" to French people.

Thumbs Up: In Australia, it is a rude gesture. In almost every other place in the world, it simply means "Okay."

Closed Fist: In some European countries, it is a gesture of contempt. In Brazil and Venezuela, it is a symbol of good luck.

BEYOND CULTURE

Cultural factors affect political systems, ideological thinking, organizational forms, and society at large. Many forces that impact the state of economy can be explained by cultural factors. For instance, part of the Japanese economic success is often attributed to Japanese culture. However, culture alone does not lead to economic depression. Governmental politics and policy, among other things, also influence the well-being of global operations. Japanese government provides a good example of the positive role of government policy in propelling its manufacturing industry to global prominence.

Forces of nature are another factor that cannot be ignored in managing global businesses. Climate patterns, natural resources, and other noncultural factors affect decisions about global businesses.

MANAGING CULTURAL DIVERSITY

A 1975 Dun's survey (1980) showed that out of the 500 largest American multinational corporations, only 87 chairmen and presidents could be considered career internationalists. Sixty-nine out of the 87 top executives had no overseas experience at all except for inspection tours. America's large domestic market and its economic success shielded the need to explore the international market. During the late 1970s and early 1980s, many American corporations found out that their market share had been eroded by foreign competitors. The parochialism of conducting business strictly from an American point of view, which was partly caused by the political, economic, and technological dominance that the U.S. enjoyed, became less and less tenable. More and more corporations realize the importance of internationalizing business operations. Organizations that operate in unfamiliar territories are sometimes surprised at the reactions of the local public to what they do. The difference in the labor union system, power structure, the makeup of the stakeholders, is all too new to even the shrewdest investors. Some local values are readily observable and some are less so to the outsiders.

Imposing the home culture onto the foreign operations and managing it strictly from a narrow point of view is often referred to as ethnocentrism. However, mindless application of popular Western management theories to other countries can lead to undesirable results. As Hofstede (1980) put it: "organizations can be culture-bound. This applies not only to the behavior of people within organizations and to the functioning of the organizations as a whole; even the theories developed to explain behavior in organizations reflect the national culture of their author, and so do the methods and techniques that are suggested for the management of organizations" (p. 372).

A different approach, which is called polycentrism, is to assume that local people know best what they should be doing, and operations is best left for the locals to handle. Geocentrism assumes all countries within the worldwide organization are equivalent. Management positions in the global organization should be based on merits regardless of race or nationality. All three approaches have their merits and shortcomings and may work well under specific cultural circumstances.

Internationalizing operations inevitably involves cultural diversity. There are advantages and disadvantages of the adoption of cultural diversity. Adler (1991) listed the advantages: multiple perspectives that derives from multiculturalism, great openness to new ideas, increasing creativity, increasing flexibility, better understanding of the foreign employees, the ability to serve the foreign customers better, and increased understanding of other cultures. Disadvantages include ambiguity, complexity, miscommunication, difficulty in reaching an agreement and agreeing on actions, and overgeneralizing organization strategies and procedures. Some of these disadvantages can be coped with by effectively managing cross-cultural communication, cross-culture teams, and diversified cultures.

Managing Cross-Cultural Communication

Cultural misperception, misunderstanding, and misevaluation could all lead to problems in an international operation where people of different cultural background, nationality, race, and language emerge together in the same organization. Ruben (1977) suggests seven skills that are necessary and important for smoothing cross-culture communication: (1) capacity to communicate respect, (2) the capacity to be nonjudgmental, (3) the capacity to accept the relativity of one's own knowledge and perceptions, (4) the capacity to display empathy, (5) the capacity to be flexible, (6) the capacity to let everyone take turns in discussions, and (7) tolerance for ambiguity.

Managing Cross-Cultural Teams

Working within a team whose members come from different cultures and exposing oneself to new cultural experiences necessarily entails a certain level of stress. It is common to miscommunicate with, misjudge, and misperceive members from other cultures, which may adversely affect both group cohesiveness and group productivity. Training is necessary to prepare people for understanding other cultures and working in diversified teams. Recognizing cultural differences, exercising mutual respect, having an open mind and a broad perspective, agreeing on an overall goal and subordinating others, emphasizing merits, and promoting team spirit are just a few ways to effectively manage cross-culture teams.

Managing Diversified Culture

In multinational operations, two cultures can often be identified: one dominant, "home" culture to which most key decision makers of the organization belong and another local culture most employees of the subsidiary and foreign facility adhere to. In some multinational corporations, the values and beliefs of the home culture are taken for granted and end up serving as a frame of reference even for persons from other cultures. There are ways to minimize possible frictions that arise out of such an organizational structure. If bilingualism and biculturalism are imposed on the foreign nationals, it is also necessary to apply the same standard to the home country executives. Creating the organization's own subculture, forming an international team where members are from different cultural background, and learning, understanding, respecting, and trying to accept each other's culture can help create cross-cultural synergy.

REFERENCES

Adler, N.J. (1991). *International Dimensions of Organizational Behavior* (2nd ed.). Belmont, CA: Wadsworth Publishing.

Axtell, R. (1993). *Do's and Taboos Around the World* (3rd ed.). New York: John Wiley & Sons.

Dun & Bradstreet, Canada, Ltd. (1980). *Canadian Book of Corporate Management*. Toronto: Dun & Bradstreet.

Fallws, J.M. (1989). More Like Us: Making America Great Again. Boston: Houghton-Mifflin.

Hofstede, G. (1980). *Culture's Consequences*. Beverly Hills: Sage Publications.

Kluckhohn, C. (1951). "Values and value-orientations in the theory of action: An exploration in definition and classification," in T. Parsons and E.A. Shils (eds.) *Towards a General Theory of Action*. Cambridge, MA: Harvard University Press.

Kroeber, A. and C. Kluckhohn (1985). *A Critical Review of Concepts and Definitions*. New York: Random House.

Myrdal, G. (1971). *Asian Drama: An Inquiry into the Poverty of Nations*. New York: Pantheon, p. 39.

Ricks, D.A. (1983). *Big Business Blunders*. Homewood, IL: Irwin.

Ruben, B. D. (1977). "Guidelines for Cross-Cultural Communication Effectiveness." *Group and Organization Studies*, 2: 470–479.

Terpstra, V. and K. David (1991). *The Cultural Environment of International Business*. Cincinnati: South-Western Publishing.

World Christian Encyclopedia. (1983). Oxford University Press.

9

Effective Global Project Management

Managers of global firms are frequently involved in projects. The planning of new plants, new products, new technologies, and quality and other training programs take a great deal of time and require detailed coordination, scheduling, and planning. Complex projects are best planned with the aid of computer software programs such as CA-Superproject, Timeline, the Harvard Total Project Manager, and Mac Project. This chapter is intended to serve as a primer in the basics of project management, so that managers can understand the theory behind the project software.

A *project* is a sequence of tasks that must be completed with an established end result. It differs from daily work in that there is a definite beginning and an ending to the sequence of tasks. When a project ends, managers and workers move on to other work or projects. Different talents are required for effective project management compared with daily managerial activities.

Projects are visible every day to the casual observer. Highways are torn up and rebuilt, shopping centers are developed, new neighborhoods created, and buildings remodeled. Rock and roll concerts, the Super Bowl, the World Cup Soccer, the Wimbledon tennis tournament, and the New York City Marathon are vast projects. Corporations engage in product development projects, nonprofit organizations undertake fund-raising projects and students tackle term projects. Managers must plan projects well in advance so that they will stay on schedule. Organization is a requirement for project managers.

Project scheduling techniques have traditionally been taught in operations management or management science courses because of the quantitative nature of these methods. These techniques, which include Gantt charts, the Critical Path Method (CPM), and the Project Evaluation and Review Technique (PERT) will be discussed in the following pages.

THE WORK BREAKDOWN STRUCTURE

The first task of project management is to identify all of the tasks (interchangeably called activities) that must be accomplished. *A work breakdown structure (WBS)* is a hierarchical relationship of the activities, divided into *project, subproject and work packages*. A WBS for the Winter Olympic Games would look something like Figure 9-1.

The project manager must break projects into manageable packages and delegate responsibilities. The next step is to establish time estimates for the activities.

The WBS in Table 9-1 outlines the actual tasks and the assigned responsibilities for the subproject within the larger project of managing the cross-country ski events.

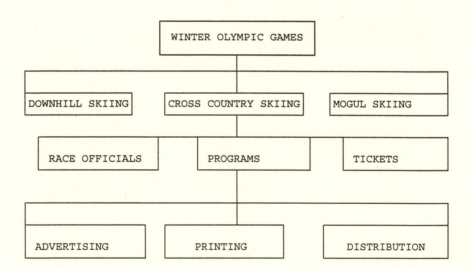

This WBS contains four levels:

Level one: Project level: Winter Olympic Games
Level two: Subproject level: Cross-Country Skiing
Level three: Task level: Programs (event brochures)
Level four: Work package: Printing

Figure 9-1 Work Breakdown Structure

Table 9–1
Work Breakdown Analysis

PROJECT: WINTER OLYMPIC GAMES
SUBPROJECT: CROSS-COUNTRY SKI RACES
PROGRAMS

Task	Work package	Responsibility
Advertising	Sales	Grace Lee
	Promotions	Kevin Arendt
	Sponsors	Jim Warlemont
Printing	Purchasing	Wendy Warlemont
	Quality Control	Johnny Angel
Distribution	Receipt	Catfish Young
	Delivery	Charley Smith

PROJECT SUCCESS FACTORS

Slevin and Pinto (1987) maintained that a successful project had ten critical success factors:

- Project Mission. The members of the project team should have a clear understanding of the purpose of the project.
- Top Management Support. The upper levels of management should communicate their support and the importance of successful project completion.
- Project Schedule/Plans. The project should not commence without a well-thought-out schedule.
- Client Consultation. Any involved clients should be actively involved in the project schedule.
- Personnel. The team should consist of the necessary personnel.
- Technical Tasks. Required technology or expertise should be available.
- Client Acceptance. Intended users should agree upon the final project.
- Monitoring and Feedback. The project's progress should be closely monitored.
- Communication. Interorganizational communications are essential to continued awareness of the project's progress.

- Trouble Shooting. Handling deviations from the schedule quickly is a desirable talent, since the only thing certain in most projects is uncertainty.

GANTT CHARTS

Henry Gantt, a Midvale Steel manager in the 1910s, developed a graphical bar chart to depict a project schedule, coincidentally called a *Gantt chart*.

Activities are listed down the vertical axis and dates are represented along the horizontal axis.

Symbols typically used include:

[Scheduled start
] Scheduled finish
___ Actual progress
X Not available
^ Current date
<> Milestone

Gantt charts are still used extensively today. Project scheduling software usually produces a Gantt chart in addition to a network flow diagram for each project. However, Gantt charts are not adequate to plan more complex projects. (See Figure 9-2)

NETWORK SCHEDULING MODELS

The need for more sophisticated project scheduling methods led to the development of two very similar networking techniques. *Project Evaluation and Review Technique (PERT)* was devised by the team planning the Polaris Missile Project in the 1950s. At the same time and without knowledge of PERT, employees at Dupont developed the *Critical Path Method (CPM)* for a complex project. Both methods rely on network precedence diagrams but differ in two ways: PERT attempts to more precisely estimate the time for each activity, whereas CPM incorporates costs into the planning spectrum. Finally, the methods proved so similar that networked project scheduling is commonly termed "PERT/CPM."

NETWORK DIAGRAMMING APPROACHES

Two diagramming approaches commonly found are the *activities-on-nodes (AON)* method and the *activities-on-arrows (AOA) method*. Either

```
Task                    Date

a.   Order programs         [__]

b.   Printing                            [_____]

c.   Check progress                                [_]      [_]

d.   Delivery                                               [-]

e.   Distribution                                          [___]

                     Aug.1 Sep.1 Oct.1 Nov.1 Dec.1 Jan.1 Feb.1

                           ^                      <>
```

Figure 9-2 Gantt Chart

method is acceptable for project scheduling, although the AON method remains easier to diagram.

AON

AON represents the activity within the box, or node, and draws an arrow between preceding and succeeding activities:

In this simple project, task A must be accomplished before task B. The completion of task B signifies the end of the project.

AOA

The activity is represented along the arrow in the AOA method, with circles signifying the beginning of one activity and the completion of another.

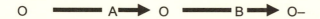

This diagram represents the same two-activity project illustrated in the AON example.

AOA vs. AON

As the complexity of a project increases, so does the network diagram. Some lines may intersect. Frequently, "dummy" activities must be added to a diagram in order to maintain the logic of the project. This is much more common to AOA diagrams than AON diagrams. AON also requires dummy nodes to connect multiple initiating or terminating activities.

Diagramming the following project and precedence relationships (see Figure 9-3):

Task	Preceded by:
A	—
B	—
C	A
D	A,B
E	C,D

Two examples of dummy activities are given. A dummy activity connects two initiating nodes, A and B, in the AON diagram and a dummy activity connects activity A's precedence to activity D in the AOA diagram.

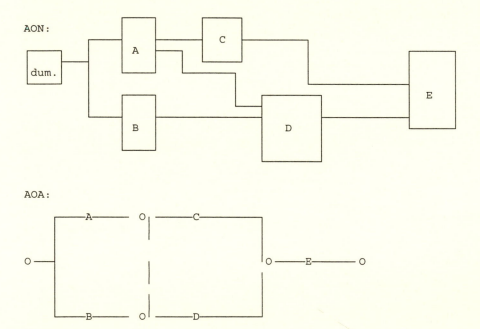

Figure 9-3 AON and AOA Networks

PROJECT SCHEDULING WITH THE CRITICAL PATH METHOD

The Critical Path Method (CPM) is a network diagram technique that involves the following steps (see Figure 9-4):

1. Identify all activities in the project.
2. Draw a network diagram that illustrates all precedence relationships of the activities.
3. Estimate the normal time to accomplish each activity.
4. Find four sets of times: the earliest start time (ES), earliest finish time (EF), the latest allowable start time (LS), and the latest allowable finish time (LF).
5. Determine the *critical path* by finding the longest path through the network.
6. The critical path is the path that determines the overall length of the project. Any attempt to reduce the project length must begin by attacking activities that are on the critical path. The critical path is also the path that exhibits the least amount of *slack*, which is excess time found along a path.

After identifying each task, estimating times, and diagramming the precedence relationship, the analyst must calculate the four times using the following procedure:

1. Earliest start times (ES). The initial node, in this case, activity A, always has an ES at time 0. Succeeding activities have an ES that is equivalent to the EF of the preceding task.

A four activity illustration of CPM, using AON:

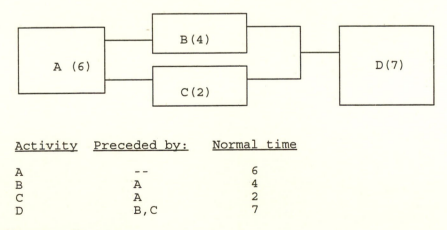

Activity	Preceded by:	Normal time
A	--	6
B	A	4
C	A	2
D	B,C	7

Figure 9-4 Critical Path Method

2. Earliest finish times (EF). The EF is found by ES + activity duration. For activity A, for example, the EF will be $0 + 6 = 6$.
3. Latest allowable start times (LS). The LS is found after all activities' ES and EF have been calculated. The terminal node, or last node (D here), will have equivalent early and late times. The LS is found by subtracting the activity duration from the late finish time (LF). For D, $17—7 = 10$.
4. Latest allowable finish times (LF). The LF is equivalent by working from the terminating node from right to left in what is called the *backward pass* through the network. An LF will be equivalent to the LS of the following, or succeeding, activity.

In the project represented in Figures 9-5 and 9-6, B and C commence simultaneously when A finishes at day 6. When two or more activities precede another activity, as in the case of B and C preceding D, the following activity can start only when both activities are finished. As a consequence, D has an ES of 10. An analogous example would be one in which you are going on a journey with two friends, but you can't leave your house until the last one arrives to start the trip.

After finding all early times, we can see that the total project time will be 17 days, since that is D's finish time.

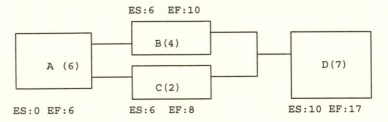

Figure 9-5 Finding Early Times

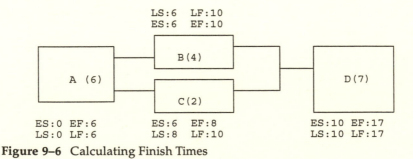

Figure 9–6 Calculating Finish Times

The late times are found by beginning at the terminal node, D. D's late times are equivalent to its early times. Moving right to left, B and C's LF times are equivalent to D's LS time, 10. To find B and C's LS, subtract the activity duration from each LF. For C: 10—2. For B: 10—4.

When we find mergers of two or more activities in the backward pass, such as both B and C merging into A, we select the LF of the preceding task by finding the lowest of the LS' of the following activities, in this case, B's 6.

Slack is detected when activities have different early and late start times. Activity C has slack because its early and late start times differ.

The critical path, the longest path and the path with the least slack, is path ABD. This path takes 17 days: A 6, B4, and D7 and has no slack, while path ACD takes 15 days and has 2 days of slack. In other words, the path ABD dictates the length of the project and to reduce that length, only a reduction in activity B will accomplish that goal.

CPM AND COSTS

Once the critical path has been determined, desirable project reductions are made using a method called "crashing." By way of introducing this approach to cost, we will review CPM by stepping through a project. (Table 9-2 and Figure 9-7)

Table 9-2
Project: New Product Development

Task	Description	Preceded By:	Normal Time
A	Product Design	—	90 DAYS
B	Market Research	—	60 DAYS
C	Prototype	A	20 DAYS
D	Market Test A	C	40 DAYS
E	Market Test B	B	40 DAYS
F	Distribution Test	C	50 DAYS
G	Quality Testing	D,E,F	90 DAYS
H	Pre-Release	G	60 DAYS
I	Advertising Prep	D,E,F	80 DAYS
J	Promotions	I	20 DAYS
K	General Release	J	20 DAYS
L	Market Research	K	40 DAYS

The network:

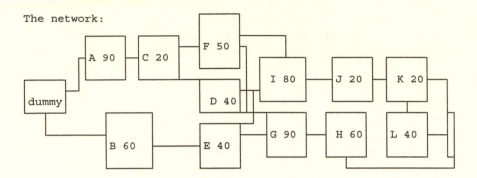

Calculating early and late times:

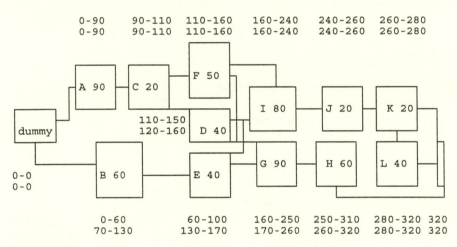

Figure 9–7(a)

The critical path is path ACFIJKL, which takes 320 days, the total length of the project. To reduce the project length, or "crash," we follow this procedure:

1. Crash only activities from the critical path.
2. Crash the activity that costs the least per day reduced.
3. Only crash activities that result in a net reduction of the total project length.
4. When dealing with multiple critical paths, all paths must be reduced simultaneously.

Task	ES	EF	LS	LF	Slack
A	0	90	0	90	0
B	0	60	70	130	70
C	90	110	90	110	0
D	110	150	120	160	10
E	60	100	130	170	70
F	110	160	110	160	0
G	160	250	170	260	10
H	250	310	260	320	10
I	160	240	160	240	0
J	240	260	240	260	0
K	260	280	260	280	0
L	280	320	280	320	0

Figure 9-7(b)

Task	Description	Preceded By:	Normal Time	Crash Time	Cost/Day
A	PRODUCT DESIGN	—	90 DAYS	80	$10,000
B	MARKET RESEARCH	—	60 DAYS	50	20,000
C	PROTOTYPE	A	20 DAYS	20	
D	MARKET TEST A	A	40 DAYS	30	60,000
E	MARKET TEST B	B	40 DAYS	30	60,000
F	DISTRIBUTION TEST	C	50 DAYS	50	
G	QUALITY TESTING	D,E,F	90 DAYS	80	30,000
H	PRE RELEASE	G	60 DAYS	50	10,000
I	ADVERTISING PREP	D,E,F	80 DAYS	60	20,000
J	PROMOTIONS	I	20 DAYS	20	
K	GENERAL RELEASE	J	20 DAYS	20	
L	MARKET RESEARCH	K	40 DAYS	30	30,000

Figure 9-7(c)

To be able to crash, we need information on the crash costs, which are the cost per day to do an activity faster. We also need to know the crash time, the fastest we can do the activity.

To reduce the project length, we must check activities that are crashable along the critical path. The least expensive activities to crash are A and I, and reducing them cuts the project length to 300 days but causes a second critical path at ACFGH.

Further reductions must attack both paths simultaneously. The top path now has only one eligible activity, L, so we must find the least expensive crashable activity to reduce at the same time from the other

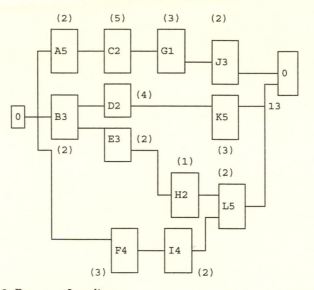

Figure 9-8 Resource Leveling

path, and that is H. Reducing H and L by 10 days each cuts the total project length to 290 days. The 30-day reduction costs $60,000.

RESOURCE LEVELING

Project managers must not only face scheduling difficulties but also the reality of constrained resources. Labor and equipment is not always available. One method for dealing with the constrained resource problem is *resource leveling*, a technique that smooths resource allocation over the length of the project, aiming to reduce period-by-period variations. (Clark and Young, 1985)

There may be a maximum level of resources available in any one period and the original allocation may exceed that level. Resource leveling does not change the amount of resources needed for individual activities, rather, it shifts the activities' early start times, taking advantage of existing slack. (See Figure 9-8 and Table 9-3)

(Resources in parentheses)

The table shows the resources for each activity by period. For example, activity A requires two resources for each of the five days needed to complete the activity. Ideally, the resources would be spread evenly across the length of the project. Figure 9-9 and Tables 9-4 and 9-5 demonstrate the actual resource usage profile compared with the ideal profile.

Table 9-3
Resource Allocation Worksheet

ACTIVITY	RESOURCE USAGE												
A	2	2	2	2	2								
B	2	2	2										
C						5	5						
D				4	4								
E				2	2	2							
F	3	3	3	3									
G								3					
H							1	1					
I					2	2	2	2					
J									2	2	2		
K						3	3	3	3	3			
L									2	2	2	2	2
TIME PER.	1	2	3	4	5	6	7	8	9	10	11	12	13
TOT RESOUR	7	7	7	11	10	12	11	9	7	7	4	2	2

Burgess and Killebrew (1962) developed a resource leveling algorithm that proceeds as follows:

1. List the activities in precedence order. Include duration and resource requirements in the proper columns.
2. List all immediately following activities. If no activities follow, place an "X" in this space.
3. Show each activity beginning at the earliest start time.
4. Total the resource usage for each time period.
5. Represent the late finish time by a small "x" across from each activity.

Resource leveling is performed by moving activities that contain slack later in the schedule and noting the resultant effect on total resources used per period. Reducing the sum of squares of the resources used is the objective. Two periods using 9 resources is preferable to one period of 8 resources and a second period of 10 resources, because $9^2 + 9^2 = 162$ and $8^2 + 10^2 = 164$.

This revised resource level smooths out the resource usage over the 13 periods. To compare the new resource levels with the previous one, sum the squares of the total resource row.

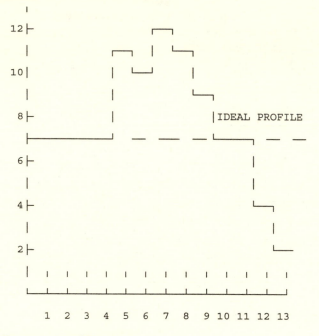

Figure 9-9 Resource Load Diagram

Table 9-4
Resource Leveling Worksheet

ACTIVITY	RESOURCE USAGE												
A-5-2-C	2	2	2	2	2		x						
B-3-2-D,E	2	2	2			x							
C-2-5-G						5	5		x				
D-2-4-K				4	4			x					
E-3-2-H				2	2	2x							
F-4-3-I	3	3	3	3x									
G-1-3-J								3		x			
H-2-1-L							1	1x					
I-4-2-L					2	2	2	2x					
J-3-2-X									2	2	2		x
K-5-3-X						3	3	3	3	3			x
L-5-2-X									2	2	2	2	2x
TIME PER.	1	2	3	4	5	6	7	8	9	10	11	12	13
TOT. RESOUR	7	7	7	11	10	12	11	9	7	7	4	2	2

Table 9-5
Revised Worksheet

ACTIVITY	RESOURCE USAGE												
A-5-2-C	2	2	2	2	2		x						
B-3-2-D,E	2	2	2			x							
C-2-5-G								5	5x				
D-2-4-K						4	4	x					
E-3-2-H				2	2	2x							
F-4-3-I	3	3	3	3x									
G-1-3-J									3x				
H-2-1-L							1	1x					
I-4-2-L				2	2	2	2x						
J-3-2-X											2	2	2x
K-5-3-X									3	3	3	3	3x
L-5-2-X									2	2	2	2	2x
TIME PER.	1	2	3	4	5	6	7	8	9	10	11	12	13
TOT. RESOUR	7	7	7	7	6	8	7	8	10	8	7	7	7

PERT

CPM treats activity duration as deterministic. PERT attempts to find a more precise estimate of the activity duration, using the formula:

$$\text{estimated time} = \frac{a + 4m + b}{6}$$

where a = optimistic time estimate

m = most likely time estimate

and b = pessimistic time estimate.

The inventors of PERT believed that individual activities took the form of the beta distribution, resulting in their choice of the formula for the estimated activity duration. It was also argued that the summing of individual activity times resulted in a normally distributed project duration, with the central limit theorem justifying the distribution.

Other authors have questioned whether the individual activities were indeed beta distributed and whether, since CPM's time estimate was the "most likely" time estimate, it is as good an estimate as any. Rather than become involved in such a serious philosophical debate, let us calculate some estimated activity times using the formula:

Activity	Optimistic	Most Likely	Pessimistic
A	6 Days	8 Days	10 Days
B	4	7	12

Time estimates:

A: $\dfrac{6 + 4(8) + 10}{6} = 8$ B: $\dfrac{4 + 4(7) + 12}{6} = 7.33$

PERT allows for the determination of the probability of completing a project on time. This requires the assumption that the individual activities are independent of each other and that the variance of the sum of the activities is normally distributed. The Z value is found by:

$Z = (D–S)/$The square root of the variance of the critical path, where:

D = desired completion time, S = total time of critical path, and Z = the number of standard deviations of the normal distribution. The variance for each activity is found by $\dfrac{(B–A)^2}{6}$.

Then, if D = 50 days
   S = 45 days
   V (variance) = 10 then $Z = (50–45)/3.16 = 1.58$ standard deviations.

From a standard Z table, we find a value of 0.9429 for a Z of 1.58. This tells us that we have a 94.29 percent probability of completing the project in 50 days or less.

PROJECT CONTROL

After a project is launched, the manager must monitor the progress of the project against time and budgeted resources. Projects have a tendency to run over-schedule and the challenge is to control the project in such a way that it is accomplished in the expected time at the expected cost.

Thamhain and Wilemon (1986) listed 30 potential problems that could lead to schedule or budget overruns:

1. Difficulty of defining work in sufficient detail.
2. Little involvement of project personnel during planning.
3. Problems with organizing and building project team.
4. No firm agreement to project plan by functional management.
5. No clear charter for key project personnel.
6. Insufficiently defined project team organization.

7. No clear role/responsibility definition for personnel.
8. Rush into project kick-off.
9. Project perceived as not important or exciting.
10. No contingency provisions.
11. Inability to measure true project performance.
12. Poor communications with upper management.
13. Poor communications with customer or sponsor.
14. Poor understanding of organizational interfaces.
15. Difficulty in working across functional lines.
16. No ties between project performance and reward system.
17. Poor project leadership.
18. Weak assistance and help from upper management.
19. Project leader not involved with team.
20. Ignorant of early warning signals and feedback.
21. Poor ability to manage conflict.
22. Credibility problems with task leaders.
23. Difficulties in assessing risks.
24. Insensitivity to organizational culture/value system.
25. Insufficient formal procedural project guidelines.
26. Apathy or indifference by project team or management.
27. No mutual trust among team members.
28. Too much unresolved/dysfunctional conflict.
29. Power struggles.
30. Too much reliance on established cost accounting system.

Thamhaim and Wilemon (1986) made a number of recommendations for improved project control, including detailed project planning, measurable milestones, commitment, intraprogram involvement, project tracking, regular reviews, communication, leadership, reward systems, senior management endorsement, and personal drive.

In summary, effective project control involves:

- A well-conceived plan
- A motivated project team
- Monitoring the activities for time and budget
- Reacting quickly to variances from the schedule or budget.

REFERENCES

Burgess, A.R. and J. B. Killebrew (1962). "Variation in Activity Level on a Cyclical Arrow Diagram." *Journal of Industrial Engineering* 13(2): 76–83.

Clark, T.B. and A.P. Young (1985). *Project Management with the Critical Path Method*. Atlanta: Young, Clark and Associates.

Slevin, D.P. and J. K. Pinto (1987). "Balancing Strategy and Tactics in Project Implementation." *Sloan Management Review*, Fall: 33–41.

Thamhain, H.J. and D. L. Wilemon (1986). "Criteria for Controlling Projects According to Plan." *Project Management Journal*, June: 75–81.

10

Technology Management for Global Operations

Operations managers must, by necessity, be technologically literate. The production of products and services requires that an operations manager possess a basic knowledge of a broad range of technology, including machinery, equipment, computers, and software. Operations managers in manufacturing industries must forecast changes in production technology and production layout, with an eye toward gaining a competitive production edge. If they have not been following technological advances, they will later be forced to spend enormous amounts of energy to learn so that they can update. Technological ignorance or naivete could result in poor decisions that could cripple a company for decades.

Among the technologies manufacturing plants may require are:

1. Materials resource planning II
2. Computer-aided design and computer-aided manufacturing
3. Expert systems
4. Robotics
5. Flexible manufacturing systems
6. Computer numerically control machine tools
7. Electronic data interchange
8. Automated materials-handling systems.

Operations managers also benefit from a number of office automation, communications technology, and software packages, including:

1. Cellular phones
2. Fax machines

3. Satellite technology
4. Modems
5. Groupware
6. Local area networks
7. Databases
8. Business application packages (spreadsheets, project management, etc.).

This chapter will review the application of these technologies to global operations.

THE TECHNOLOGY MANAGER

Whether an operations manager works for a bank or for an auto manufacturer, the major issue is the effective production and delivery of the product to the customer. Each industry has its own technological production peculiarities and options, which astute managers know, and understand.

The issues of technological choice include cost, speed, quality, space allocation, obsolescence potential, experience of the machine manufacturer, number of other users, customer service, maintenance costs, maintenance speed, dependability, and ease of use. Few manufacturers have the capabilities to design and build their own assembly lines or machine tools and must contract specialty manufacturers for that purpose.

Cost is often the most decisive factor in the technology purchase decision, but it should not be. Machine purchase considerations must factor maintenance costs, service costs, serviceability, delivery, and output capabilities into the final decision.

Speed is the cycle-time of the technology. For example, a laser printer may print at 6 pages per minute, and cost $900. A printer with a speed of 4 pages per minute may cost $600. Service costs for both printers are virtually nil, and repairs are available within 24 hours. The issue: is it ever critical to get a document out so fast that the speed becomes important? If the need is typically for 100 page documents, the faster printer can save 8 minutes in production time. This printer example is analogous to the typical production equipment choice: some machines have greater capacity and speed capabilities, and the determination of which machine to buy depends on volume and need for responsiveness. One job alone may justify the additional expense of a faster machine if it delivers a product to market when the customer wants it.

The quality of the technology may take several forms: durability, reliability, features, performance, and conformance are all important quality aspects of technology. How long will it last, given a certain amount of use? What is its service record? Repairability? Does it offer features that will improve the quality and speed of delivery? What are the technology's performance characteristics? How well does the product conform to specifications?

Space considerations may dictate that certain technologies simply do not fit into an existing location. Some equipment may require special ventilation or environmental considerations. This all seems like common sense, yet there are many stories of purchased equipment that cannot fit through existing doors. For example, a husband and wife contracted for a new house, and when it was completed, discovered that the garage was not tall enough for their recreational vehicle (RV). Rather than sell the RV, or build a new garage, the final solution was to let the air out of the tires every time the RV was parked. Plants have similar horror stories.

Determining the potential for obsolescence requires a knowledge of emerging technologies. It is always dangerous to invest in a mature technology A, when technology B is available to purchase. This comes down to betting on which technology will be the most useful in the coming years. Betting on the wrong technology may leave a company with equipment that someday will be devoid of service and parts.

The experience of the machine manufacturer is a very important factor in the purchase of technology. How long has the manufacturer been out there with their products, serving existing customers? What is the level of customer satisfaction? Mercedes-Benz sells this fact to buyers: We have been here a long time—years longer than Lexus and Infiniti.

The number of other users, and their relative locations, are important information that tells not only the popularity of the equipment but also that the local sales commitment should be backed up with an accompanying service network. It pays to contact a vendor's users for a service report card, before signing a purchase contract. It is especially a concern when there is a great geographic distance between the vendor and the plant.

Simplicity and ease of use are good reasons to select one technology over another. User-friendly technology enables faster returns to normal productivity when machine operators change. Learning curves for technology can be quite steep, and the easier the equipment is to operate, the more workers can be trained to operate.

MANUFACTURING TECHNOLOGIES

The various technologies required to run a manufacturing firm are sometimes grouped under an umbrella term, "Computer Integrated

Manufacturing," (CIM). CIM, for the most part, remains pie-in-the-sky. The implementation of many manufacturing technologies is often done halfway, and integration is not possible until all systems are operational and mastered. Wobbe (1990) argued against European adoption of CIM, due to CIM's absence of a human-centered, skill-based approach to manufacturing.

Key manufacturing technologies include:

Materials resource planning II (MRP II). At the heart and soul of many manufacturer's planning tools is the MRP system. MRP is the dependent demand inventory system that plans the inventory needs of all parts "exploding" from a "parent" product. Although MRP has been available since the 1970s, many companies have yet to master the software. If an MRP system is to become fully operational and successful, it must be properly implemented, and that is perhaps the most difficult stage of MRP. The implementation of all the MRP modules takes more than a year, and must be done while daily work continues. Existing inventory systems must continue to run, while product information is entered into the several databases running the MRP system.

Those companies that successfully implement MRP reap many financial and planning benefits from the system. If the software fits the inventory management scheme for a company, and the number of products is sufficiently complex, MRP is well worth the investment.

Some MRP systems fail because they are never fully installed. Others find that there is not enough time to work on the installation while keeping the company going, and top management does not make a full commitment to the installation. The systems are very expensive to buy, and often require additional labor and educational costs to get going, but once they are operational, companies should receive a fair payback on their investment.

Computer-aided design and computer-aided manufacturing (CAD-CAM). CAD-CAM ties together the computer design with computerized manufacturing. CAD has greatly reduced the product design cycle time, but the majority of firms have yet to turn on the switch connecting CAD to CAM.

Mosher and Majchrzak (1986) discovered that the actual integration of CAD to CAM was not the biggest cause of increased coordination between design and manufacturing. Rather, it was the organizational factors such as management's encouragement for collaboration that enhanced coordination.

Expert systems. Expert systems are a form of artificial intelligence in which a computer program is written that models the decisions of experts for certain applications. Such systems are growing rapidly in use, and have many advantages. Badiru (1992) listed eight major benefits for developing an expert system to solve a problem:

1. Expert systems increase the probability, frequency, and consistency of making good decisions.
2. Expert systems help distribute human expertise.
3. Expert systems facilitate real-time, low-cost, expert-level decisions by the non-expert.
4. Expert systems enhance the utilization of most of the available data.
5. Expert systems permit objectivity by weighing evidence without bias and without regard for the user's personal and emotional reactions.
6. Expert systems permit dynamism through modular of structure.
7. Expert systems free up the mind and time of the human expert to enable him or her to concentrate on more creative activities.
8. Expert systems encourage investigations into the subtle areas of a problem (p. 22).

Expert systems have found a number of applications for operations, including:

1. Maintenance. Like a physician, a maintenance expert system can review a number of problem symptoms and prescribe a number of alternative solutions.
2. Facility location. Expert systems can be programmed to include heuristics, or rules for locating a plant or building, and design the interior layout.
3. Inventory management. Decisions on order quantities, and inventory stocking policies can be modeled with an expert system, and take much of the guesswork out of inventory decision-making.
4. Scheduling. Labor and machine scheduling are areas often benefiting from an expert system. An expert system could reduce the possibility of a new manager not understanding the scheduling methods of the predecessor.
   Other areas with manufacturing applications for expert systems include flexible manufacturing system design, robotics, and materials handling (Badiru, 1992).
5. Robotics. Robotics take many forms but are most appropriate for repetitive and physically dangerous jobs. Robots have the obvious advantage of reliability and consistency over humans—assuming minimal maintenance, they don't go on strike or call in sick.
6. Flexible manufacturing systems. FMSs were found in one British study (Haywood and Bessant, 1990) to reduce lead times by 74

percent, reduce work in progress inventory by 68 percent, increase inventory turnover by 350 percent and increase machine utilization by 63 percent.

These systems employ automated materials handling within a work station connected to a centralized computer which provides instructions for routing jobs (Render and Helzer, 1994).

Because of the flexibility advantages, many manufacturers have either adopted or are considering this technology.

7. Computer numerically controlled machine tools. These are the popular form in machining, due to the increased reliability of precision a computer program can provide. This technology was invented in the United States, but popularized by the Japanese, as noted in an earlier chapter.

8. Simulation. Simulation offers a tool to experiment with plant layouts and scheduling algorithms, which does not interfere with the actual plant processes. Computer simulation modelers graphically represent a plant, enabling plant managers to tinker and make mistakes, looking for optimal approaches.

Operations managers also benefit from a number of office automation and software packages, including cellular phones, fax machines, satellite technology, modems, groupware, local area networks, databases, electronic data interchange (EDI), business application packages, and electronic mail. The effect these technologies have on the operations manager is to reduce the distance among plants. The days of one week delivery of important correspondence being sent across the world have faded into the past. Today, communication across the globe is up-to-the-minute.

E-mail has changed the way managers communicate. Rather than writing letters and sending memos, fast responses by E-mail speed the communication channels. Taking E-mail one step further, groupware allows communication with a greater number of network users (Kirkpatrick, 1993). Memos are sent to a bulletin board and network users may pick from the board all correspondences they desire to read. "Lotus Notes" is the bestselling groupware package, enabling thousands of people to tie into the system. Dell Computer, for example, ties 1,125 employees together through Lotus Notes.

EDI was a major advance for buyer-supplier relationships in the 1970s. First offered through stand-alone printers and modems, and later through personal computers, EDI changed many purchasing practices. The buyer directly interfaces the supplier's warehouse inventory system and receives on-line information on availability and price. After checking for availability, a manager transmits a purchase order by modem. If Supplier A is out-of-stock on an item, supplier B's warehouse might be checked, rather than back-order the item. EDI helped purchasing agents reduce stockouts. The day of the telephoned purchase order is a thing of the past for most major corporations.

INTRODUCING NEW TECHNOLOGIES

One thing all technology has in common is the difficulty of implementation. Change brings with it a human cost. Not only must workers learn new ways to work, they must sometimes go through an arduous period of adjustment to new technologies.

Personal computers are a generally accepted tool of management. Still, many managers of today never took the time to learn how to use a personal computer. It is inexcusable for managers attempting to introduce new technologies to their work force when they haven't even bothered to personally master new technology.

Ann Majchrzak (1988) described first-order effects of new technology on the human infrastructure. These include changes to the nature of the work of equipment operators, technical and administrative support personnel, managers, and supervisors. Job changes include the increased need for coordination and information.

Second-order effects are changes in skill requirements, selection, training, personnel policies, and organizational structure. Majchrzak (1988) designed a human infrastructure impact statement (HIIS) to delineate all of the change aspects of new technology. Her statement contained impacts on job activities, technical support functions, management functions, supervisory functions, skill requirements, selection, training, personnel policies, and organizational structure.

An impact analysis should actually be conducted before the purchase of new technology, to estimate the potential for disruption of productivity, and then studied closely, during, and after implementation. A successful transition from one technology to another usually requires the acceptance of key line workers, those informal leaders and opinion shapers of the line. If a project team analyzes the potentials of new technology, these line leaders should be included in team membership.

INFORMATION TECHNOLOGY

As we have demonstrated in the above, most of the technologies used in manufacturing can be called information technology. For instance, as their names indicate, CAD and CAM store manufacturing data electronically, share databases among production, marketing, engineering, and sales departments, and design and manufacture through the aid of computer software. Recently, there is a clear trend towards integrating information technology into manufacturing. The wide use of materials requirements planning software exemplifies this trend. However, different countries may place different priorities in the adoption of the various types of information technology in manufacturing.

On the basis of the survey reported by de Meyer and Ferdows (1985), companies in Japan, United States, and some European countries (UK, France, Germany, Belgium, Italy, Spain, Sweden, the Netherlands, Switzerland, Denmark, and Norway) have put different priorities on the use of information systems in manufacturing.

The most emphasized information systems by European companies are quality control, strategic planning, sales forecasting, sales planning and analysis, and materials requirements planning. The priority order for U.S. companies is quality control, inventory status, master production scheduling, materials requirements planning, and shop floor control. Japanese companies emphasize quality control, cost accounting, shop floor control, master production scheduling, and process control. One commonality is the universal importance of high quality. The differences lie in that European companies tend to put more focus on sales planning and forecasting, U.S. companies on materials management, and Japanese companies on cost accounting and process control.

The use of information technology in manufacturing may differ from region to region. U.S. companies are concerned with integrating the information of materials flow into manufacturing, Japanese companies focus on process information, and European companies emphasize sales information in manufacturing planning.

CONCLUSIONS

Technology has two sides—the product side and the process side. A firm must be selling the right technology and using the right technology. Managers must play the part of prognosticator to predict technology. The more the manager knows about the advantages and disadvantages of different technologies, the more apt the manager will be to bet on the right technology. This prognosticator role of the operations manager requires a great deal of technical learning. Operations managers must do an enormous amount of research to stay one step ahead of technology.

Global operations managers must inventory their production processes across the globe. It may be perfectly justifiable to use an outdated technology in a plant whose sole role is to supplement capacity. A good deal of planning and capital budgeting is necessary to make sure that all plants don't become obsolete at the same time. The ability to update all plants simultaneously is dependent on the available number of skilled people to help implementation. An inventory of available personnel for technology implementation project teams will dictate the speed of changeover. If a company has six plants across the globe, and two complete project teams, this will obviously inhibit the speed of global transition.

Office automation has improved so rapidly that information flow across the world is up-to-the-minute. This also has the by-product of diminishing the installation of new process technology. Product design cycles have shrunken since the advent of CAD-CAM, again assisting in reduced cycle times for process technology changes. Still, the difficulty of getting the most out of information systems such as MRP, is that information must be coded while the work gets done, and time is a precious commodity. An investment in a temporary work force, or consulting assistance, may appear costly up front, but be of tremendous value in getting the new technology installed correctly. A good rule is to never scrimp on postinstallation training. There are many cases of firms who chose to send only a few key people for training, with the intention that these people would then apply the same training to their fellow employees. This is a big risk because some of these trained people may leave the company before the training is completed, or their daily work becomes more important to them than their training, so they postpone the training.

A review of the lightning-like changes in technology in the past decade proves that the operations manager is on a sort of bucking bronco. If the operations manager is to tame the bronco, he or she must know and have a way with horses. The surest way to get tossed off the bronco is to not pay attention. And that is the message of this chapter: Read and study technologies. Know about them in advance.

REFERENCES

Badiru, A. B. (1992). *Expert Systems Applications in Engineering and Manufacturing.* Englewood Cliffs, NJ: Prentice-Hall.

de Meyer, A. and K. Ferdows (1985). "Integration of Information Systems in Manufacturing." *International Journal of Operations and Production Management,* 5:5–12.

Haywood, B., and J. Bessant (1990). "Organisation and Integration of Production Systems," in M. Warner, W. Wobbe, and P. Brodner (eds.), *New Technology and Manufacturing Management.* Chichester, West Sussex, United Kingdom: John Wiley & Sons.

Kirkpatrick, D. "Groupware Goes Boom." *Fortune,* December 27, 1993, pp. 99–104.

Majchrzak, A. (1988). *The Human Side of Factory Automation.* San Francisco: Jossey-Bass.

Mosher, P. and A. Majchrzak (1986). "Workplace Changes Mediating Effect of Technology on Individuals' Attitudes and Performance." Presented at the Academy of Management. Chicago.

Render, B. and J. Heizer (1994). *Principles of Operations Management*. Boston: Allyn & Bacon.

Wobbe, W. (1990). "A European View of Advanced Manufacturing in the United States," in M. Warner, W. Wobbe, P. and Brodner (eds.), *New Technology and Manufacturing Management*. Chichester, West Sussex, United Kingdom: John Wiley & Sons.

11

Managing International Service Operations

A lot has been written about why service management is different and unique from manufacturing and why it requires its own literature. The intangibility and heterogeneity of service products makes service management quite a different experience than dealing with the inventory and distribution of finished goods. The following table points out that as economies mature, the percentage of service employment increases.

Included within service employment is governmental employment. In the United States, for example, close to 10 percent of the workforce are governmental workers. As service employment increases, manufacturing and agricultural employment naturally decrease.

Most service companies across the world are small, local businesses, with fewer than 10 employees. However, the large, global service firms are in intensely competitive industries: airlines, delivery services, hotels, banking, construction, shipping, credit cards, and fast-food restaurant chains.

Chase (1981), an early researcher in service operations management, hypothesized that there was an inverse relationship between a customer's involvement in the production system, and productivity. He developed what he called a "customer contact" model, in which potential facility efficiency is given as a function of 1 minus the customer contact time divided by the service creation time.

Schmenner (1993) classified services according to four groups: the service factory, the service shop, mass service, and professional service. A service factory is the service version of an assembly line, with low labor intensity and a low degree of interaction and customization. Low-cost services such as no-frills airlines and no-frills supermarkets

Table 11–1

Changes in % of Service Employment

	France	Germany	Japan	Neth.	U.K.	USA
1960–1973	7.2	9.5	11.7	10.1	6.6	5.3
1973–1985	10.4	8.1	8.0	9.8	9.9	5.9
1985 %	61.9	54.3	57.0	67.5	65.3	72.2

(Sources: Elfring, T., "New evidence on the expansion of service employment in advanced economies," *The Service Industries Journal*, 9, 337–56, and Daniels, P.W., *Service Industries in the World Economy*, 1993. Blackwell: Oxford, United Kingdom).

are examples. A service shop is a service version of a job shop, with a high degree of interaction and customization and a low degree of labor intensity. Examples are hospitals and restaurants.

A mass service features a high degree of labor intensity and a low degree of interaction and customization. Examples are retail establishments and commercial banking. A professional service has a high degree of interaction and customization and a high degree of labor intensity. Law firms and consulting firms are examples of the professional service.

Each type of service brings a different approach to service delivery. A no-frills airline would want to minimize customer services and find ways to increase customer involvement in the production system. Some supermarkets have succeeded by reducing their prices and having the customers bag their own groceries.

Albrecht and Zemke (1985) credit Scandinavia as being as much pioneers to service management as Japan was pioneers to manufacturing management. Jan Carlzon, the CEO for the Scandinavia Airline System (SAS) turned around a struggling airline by concentrating his company on serving their customers. Carlzon noted that the service encounter between employee and customer is the "moment of truth," in which the image and reputation of the company is being conveyed by the employee. Albrecht and Zemke comment:

> "Since managers cannot be there to influence the quality of so many moments of truth, they must learn to manage them indirectly, that is, by creating a customer-oriented organization, a customer-friendly system as well as a work environment that reinforces the idea of putting the customer first." (p. 27).

THE RAW MATERIAL OF SERVICES

In a manufacturing system, the inputs to production are raw materials such as glass, steel, or plastic. The production managers are responsible for planning and forecasting production, inventory management, purchasing, layout and location, managing projects, and scheduling labor and production. This system produces a finished good. Quality is the feedback mechanism for defective finished goods—flaws are returned to the system.

A service version of this system takes a customer as the raw material. Virtually the same activities are carried out by a service operations manager and a manufacturing production manager.

The "finished" service also has a quality feedback loop. If the service is not correctly transacted, the customer will either complain or not return to the service.

One service example is a university, where the inputs to an undergraduate program are high school graduates. The university "production managers" make sure that classes are scheduled, rooms assigned, and faculty matched with courses and classrooms. The system provides the educational tools (computers, blackboards, VCRs, televisions, overhead projectors, etc.) that professors need to teach their students. The students are presented with material and tested on their mastery. There is evidence of quality at work throughout the system:

1. Admissions is a quality checkpoint that admits only students who have earned their places at the school.
2. Testing is a quality checkpoint that makes sure the students have mastered the course materials.
3. Teacher evaluations are quality checks that make sure the instruction has accomplished the intended goals.
4. The ultimate quality checkpoint is the job performance of the graduates; if graduates of a university do not do well in the work place, eventually the reputation of the university will suffer.

Another service example is the fast-food restaurant. Here, the raw materials are hungry customers. They come into the operations system, where a properly configured operations will have matched the labor schedule with demand periods, and an efficient method for preparing food has been devised. If all operations are done correctly, the customer's state is changed from hungry to satisfied, and that is the end output of this service system. Once again, a series of quality checkpoints are in place.

1. The operations system should have inspection points built in to make sure the food is properly prepared.
2. The customer may detect a problem with the quality of the food, or the quality of the service, and make their displeasure known. At these times, the restaurant is on alert. It is a time of customer retrieval, and out-of-the ordinary service is called for.

3. Bad quality may go undetected, and when it does, it may or may not be reported. Various estimates have placed the number of people a customer tells about poor quality as anywhere from 7 to 15.

Given that a service operations system is designed to transform a customer's state, the challenge for global services is to provide consistent quality across geographical boundaries. That may be easier for a financial service firm than a restaurant chain. The restaurant chain must select sources of supply that meet their standards, and that may be difficult in some regions of the world. Tastes differ, also, so some menu variations must be addressed, offering additional potential to compromise quality.

Global services must think locally to succeed. What works for the Marriott Hotel in New York City might fail in London. The formula that works in one region should be market-tested in another before implementation. Truly good service companies eventually lose their geographical identity, and are thought of as a local company that employs many locals.

SERVICE PRODUCTIVITY AND QUALITY

The difficulty in measuring service productivity has always been in defining the output, establishing standards and measurable parameters, and dealing with the customer's perception of service performance. Service outputs are often very intangible. Take one example of a hard-to-measure service—an office of psychiatrists. An obvious output measure for a team of psychiatrists would be revenue per hour, but that says nothing about the effectiveness of treatments. They would be very concerned with the productivity of their billing department—the average number of days it takes to receive payment. Psychiatrists have the very real problem of having a hard time knowing if they have completely transformed their "troubled client" into a "healthy client." If the client suddenly stops coming to the office, it may be that they can no longer afford the services or they do not think they are getting anything out of the treatment. Perhaps the best option for a psychiatrists' office is to use marketing research tools to detect the level of satisfaction with their services both for current and former clients.

Any meaningful measures of the service output must take customers' needs and requirements into consideration. Quinn (1992) suggests several service-based productivity focus shifts. First is a shift from individual product profitability to the total profitability from the customer relationship. Second is a move from short-term transaction measures to long-term customer outcome measures. Next is a reorientation from internal cost performance criteria to external performance measures based on customer perceptions. Last is a change from focus on structurally-orientated indicators to focus on process-oriented indicators of how well tasks are performed.

The productivity measurement system should be aimed at the intended desired output of the service. An attorney's office may be so focused on increasing one productivity measurement, "billable hours," that they neglect other tasks important to the firm's long-term survival, that is, prospecting, researching, and filing. All service organizations should develop a productivity and quality measurement system, monitor the reports, and emphasize to employees the importance of the results.

There are a number of management approaches that can be used to improve service productivity.

1. Establishing a balance of customization and standardization. Certain service elements should be standardized in order to control variations in service delivery and to reduce costs. Other service elements should be customized to meet individual customer requirements. The appropriate level of standardization depends on the service firm's strategy, market niche, and its competitors' reaction.

2. Automating service production and delivery processes. Replacing people with machines is a standard productivity enhancement that has been used in the service industries. ATMs, electronic funds transfer systems, optical mail scanners, and CAT scanners are just a few examples of automation in the service sector. Automation enables service companies to provide fast and reliable services and, in the long run, reduce operating costs.

3. Achieving a balance between economies of scale and diseconomies of scale. Hospitals have valuable facilities, equipment, and instruments that require large investment. Large hospitals can make full use of their fixed assets and allow for the spread of the fixed cost to many patients, thus lowering the unit cost per patient. However, when hospitals expand to a certain level, scale economies may no longer hold and diseconomies appear. Difficulty in managing the large scale facility and overseeing comprehensive service offerings eventually outweighs the benefits of scale economies.

4. Utilizing assistants to do supportive work. Many professions require special training and knowledge and these professionals are usually highly paid. Asking them to perform routine tasks that can be easily performed by their assistants can be a waste of money and time. For instance, the basic case research can be conducted by legal interns under the direction of a lawyer. Filling out a patient information sheet can be

done by a nurse or medical assistant before the patient sees a doctor. In this way, lawyers and doctors can do what they are good at and increase their productivity.

5. Managing demand. Since service cannot be inventoried, there is the potential of a mismatch of demand and supply. Fast-food outlets are fully utilized during lunch hours and less crowded in other times. A golf course can be idle and busy based on the weather, season, and time of day. To improve the utilization of facility and the productivity of service providers, many service companies require appointment system to even out the demand.

6. Training employees. Competent employees are the cornerstone of any business success. Training employees and equipping them with skills and knowledge that they need to perform the tasks efficiently is the key to increasing labor productivity. Tough competition and pressure for cutting cost often lead service firms to hire more part-timers to replace full-time employees. Without proper training of the part-timers, this type of cost cutting may result in customer dissatisfaction, and soon enough, the firms may find themselves losing customers. Having qualified employees and striking a balance between full-time and parttime employees pay off in the long run.

7. Allowing customers to perform some of the service. Self-service in gas stations is quite common. Asking the customers to bus their own table after lunch and requesting clients to organize their receipts before the accountant files tax forms can increase service providers' productivity.

Managing for productivity is important. However, a focus on short-term productivity may actually lead to poorer service quality and cause customer dissatisfaction.

Zeithaml, Parasuraman, and Berry (1990) categorized service quality into 10 dimensions:

1. Tangibles—the appearance of physical facilities, appearance of personnel.
2. Reliability—the ability to perform the promised service consistently.
3. Responsiveness—the ability to respond promptly to customers.
4. Competence—the adequate knowledge and skills of the workers.
5. Courtesy—the politeness of the employees toward customers.
6. Credibility—the "believability" of the server.
7. Security—the comfort the customer feels in the server's locale.
8. Access—the ease of access to the service.
9. Communication—listening and communicating with customers.
10. Understanding the customer—knowing the customer's expectations and wants.

The customer's expectations are critical determinants to service quality. Zeithaml, Parasuraman, and Berry (1990) defined quality "gaps" as the difference between management's perceptions of customer expectations and the actual customer expectations. Every customer enters a service encounter with certain expectations. The service's ability to meet those expectations will determine the customer's perception of quality.

Customers know what to expect when they go to McDonald's restaurants. In fact, most customers can taste a McDonald's french fry in the taste buds of their memory. McDonald's extensive efforts to provide consistent product go a long way toward setting expectations.

Nordstrom's department store has achieved a reputation for serving the customer that raises the customer's expectations any time they come into the store. Service managers have to understand customer's expectations. If they expect a low-cost, no-frills service and they encounter higher prices, the quality image will suffer. Southwest Airlines has succeeded with that very strategy, forcing larger airlines to reduce prices in competitive markets.

TECHNOLOGY IN SERVICES

The omnipresence of technology has dramatically shaped the structure of the service industry and impacted service performance. No longer is the service sector viewed as low capital and low technology. Imaging devices, CAT scanners, fetal monitors, life-support system, surgical procedures have revolutionized medical practices; Electronic funds transfer systems, automatic teller machines, and pneumatic delivery systems have enabled financial institutions to perform more efficiently and effectively; Automatic retrieval systems, containerization, loading, and refrigeration have changed material-handling systems. Wide applications of electronics, information, and communications technologies have stimulated new innovation in virtually all service areas.

Major new technologies in services generate certain distinctive patterns, as pointed out by Guile and Quinn (1988). The first pattern is that small facilities or units in more dispersed locations can link into networks with large companies to take advantage of new economies of scale. This pattern is seen in health care, insurance, banking and financial services, and communications. The second trend is that the same technologies that created new scale economies allow service firms to handle a much wider set of data, output functions, and customers without significant cost increases. Banks, airlines, and retailers use their networks to expand businesses into a broader range of new services.

The third feature is that increased complexity can be handled by the new technologies. One example is that, equipped with new technologies, medical communities are able to perform more complicated procedures and treat patients with rare diseases.

Information technology is most common and critical in service industries. A lot of service innovations came of age with the aid of information technology. There are three stages in the adoption of an information technology in service industries (Barras, 1986). The first stage is the application of the new technology designed to increase the efficiency of delivery of existing services. Take insurance and accountancy as examples. The mainframe computer allowed insurance companies to computerize policy records and accounting firms to do computer audit and internal time recording. The next stage involves the use of technology to improve service quality. On-line systems permit insurance companies to access on-line policy quotations and accounting firms to computerize management accounting systems. The last stage begins when technology is utilized to assist in generating new services. Insurance companies offer complete on-line service and accounting firms extend fully automated auditing and accounting systems. Information technology has shaped the structure of the service industry, increased the relative power of service businesses, and presented great opportunities and challenges for service companies. Those who ignore or are not prompt to seize the opportunities that are created by technology generally lose their competitive advantages.

Technology has made it possible for service firms to provide a wider array of services more efficiently than they could before. However, as technology becomes a part of standard delivering service, personal interaction becomes more important in satisfying customers and in differentiating competitors. Managers must be aware of the potential changes brought about by technology on service operations. Some work may become more conceptual and challenging and require greater skills and knowledge. Since new technology often eliminates certain jobs or replaces old jobs with new, more challenging ones, some workers may not be able to make the transition and face unemployment, while others have to be retrained and relearn new skills (Collier, 1983).

SERVICE FOCUS

No business can be everything to everyone. Davidow and Uttal (1989) give two examples to illustrate the impact of service focus on performance. One successful example is the Shouldice Hospital near Toronto. This hospital treats only one type of patient—those with a hernia. They reject hernia patients who have a history of heart trouble or who have undergone surgery in the first 12 months. Patients go to the operating room on their own, walk to the recovery room, and take their meals in a common dining room. Patients also pay less. Doctors are highly proficient and productive in this specialty area. The hospital's service strategy is very focused and its market segment is clearly defined. In contrast, the airline People Express pursued conflicting strategies. In 1981, People Express focused exclusively on budget travelers who were willing to sacrifice convenience and service for low fares. They grew rapidly, but overexpanded. Since budget travelers fly mainly during weekends, they decided to attract business travelers during weekdays. Their existing practices that serve budget commuters were in conflict with the new strategy. Business people disliked the inconvenient schedules and paying extras for meals and baggage check-in. The airline had a $300 million net loss in 1986. These two examples indicate that the essence of the service focus is to find the right mix of service offerings and to segment customers.

Given limited resources, it is in the best interest of service companies to concentrate their efforts on the service that they are good at and their target customers care about. Fuzzy or conflicting service strategies make good customer service impossible.

SERVICE RECOVERY

Serving customers is the quintessential reason for the existence of businesses. Service firms spend a lot of money attracting new customers. However, they sometimes ignore existing customers. Most firms focus on costs and revenues and overlook the expected cash flow a loyal customer could bring over an entire life span. For instance, in the credit card business, a company has to spend $51 to recruit a new customer and set up an account. The expected profit from the first-year customer is $30, but for a fifth-year customer it is $55 (Reichheld and Sasser, 1990). Another reason is that service employees are usually rewarded by how many new customers they attract and how many new accounts they open, instead of how many old customers they retain. Customer loyalty drives profitability through repeated purchases, reduced operating costs, and free referral services. It is estimated that companies can boost profits by almost 100 percent by retaining just 5 percent more of their existing customer base (Reichheld and Sasser, 1990).

Service organizations occasionally make mistakes or mistreat a customer. When this happens, they are in peril of losing the customer forever. Consequently, an extraordinary effort for service recovery is called for, not only to recapture the customer but also to impress the customer so much that they tell all of their friends about the experience.

The attitude that "the customer is always right" guides the employees to proper service. Of course, some customers will lie, cheat, or even steal, and that is why services have security people and fraud divisions. However, a service cannot succeed with an inherent distrust of its customers. Many a service employee has muttered the phrase, "This job would be pretty good if it wasn't for the customers!" The truth is that they would have no job if it wasn't for the customers.

While the service providers may not be able to avoid all mistakes, they can learn to recover from them. A good service recovery can turn a disgruntled customer into a loyal one and turn a frustrating experience into a fond memory. One way to enhance service recovery is to allow the front-line employees to identify problems and empower them to correct service mistakes. Sometimes, employees are frustrated because they do not have the power to make decisions and solve the problems. Every customer's problem can be turned into an opportunity for the company to show its commitment to service and customers. Hart and his colleagues (1990) point out some practical guidelines for service recovery.

Anticipate Needs for Recovery

New services have a tendency to create confusion and unexpected requests. New employees are inexperienced and tend to make errors related to unfamiliarity with the system.

Act Fast

Identifying the problem and correcting it before the customer complains can certainly eliminate the possibility of registering a bad experience in the customer's mind. Responding to the customer's complaint and acting quickly to correct the mistake can also show the service provider's promptness and sense of responsibility.

Train Employees

Proper training of employees can eliminate a lot of service errors. Training should focus not only on how to perform tasks but also on how to recover service errors.

Empower the Front Line

Training gives employees skills required for service recovery. The company must give the front-line employees the power to make decisions and to correct mistakes. In some cases, the employees have identified the mistakes but do not have the authority to correct mistakes immediately.

Close the Loop

If the company has fixed a problem that the customer complained about, it should inform the customer of the improvements. If the company cannot fix the problem, it should also let the customer know why. This is called "closing the loop" to make the customer feel that their suggestions are taken seriously and the company is genuinely committed to service.

SERVICE GUARANTEE

When you buy a product, it usually comes with a warranty. When you buy a service, you rarely get a warranty. While services are often perceived as more risky and uncertain than products, it makes sense to have service assurance.

Products can be inspected before being shipped to the customer. When something goes wrong, in most cases it can be repaired. On the other hand, the simultaneous production and consumption of services and the intangible nature of the service make inspection before selling impossible. How can the customer preinspect a haircut, or how can the doctor inspect a surgical operation before it starts? The intangibility of services makes service specifications hard to define. Customer involvement and participation in the service process create more variability. Therefore, many service firms believe that service guarantee is infeasible.

Fimstahl (1989) provides a real-life example of service guarantee in a restaurant business. As an owner of a chain of four restaurants, he expressed his promise as *"Your Entertainment Guaranteed. Always,"* abbreviated as YEGA. This promise became their driving force and was included in all advertising, printed brochures, letterhead, and menus. This promise is not an empty slogan. Several steps are taken to implement this service guarantee. Every employees is required to sign a contract to implement YEGA. Employees are empowered to do anything to keep the customer happy. Any employee can provide a complementary wine or dessert when delays or errors occur. Correction does cost money! The cost of keeping the service promise is not just the price tag for the service guarantee, the owner viewed it as a cost of system failures. As Fimstahl (1989) put it: "Costs will go up before they come down, so high system-failure costs and low phone-survey complain rates probably mean you are on the right track" (p. 31) and "As long as you offer an absolute guarantee on your products and services, you will incur system-failure costs. There is always more work to do, and a CEO's personal commitment and persistence are often necessary to get it done. But motivated employees are essential" (p. 32).

A good service guarantee should be unconditional, easy to understand and communicate, meaningful, easy to invoke, and easy and quick to collect on (Hart, 1988).

SERVICE GAFFES AND HURRAHS

Successful service companies herald those moments of legendary service: the Delta Airlines employee who runs through the airport to give a passenger his forgotten briefcase, the Federal Express employee who rents a helicopter to repair a downed transmission line, and the Nordstrom employee who includes several shirts and ties with a suit that was late being altered. More often than not, such episodes go unreported unless the customer takes the time to write about it. Similarly, most moments of poor service go unreported.

Waiting Line Management

Queue management is a critical aspect of many service operations. A number of formulas can be used to determine the optimal number of servers. To calculate the formulas, one must know the rate at which customers arrive into the "system," and the rate at which servers can serve customers. These rates are usually expressed in number per time period.

If a = the average number of arrivals per time period.
and b = the average number of customers served per time period.

the formulas for a one-line system are:

Average number of customers in the system = $a/b\text{-}a$
This tells the average number both being served and in the waiting line.

Average time in the system = $1/b\text{-}a$
This formula tells how long it takes to wait plus be served.

Average number of customers in the queue = $a^2/b(b\text{-}a)$
This tells how many customers are in the entire line, on the average.

Average customer waiting time $= a/b(b-a)$

How long does a customer wait before being served, on the average?

Utilization factor $= a/b$

This formula is the waiting line's productivity factor, telling the percent of time the line is in use.

Multiple waiting line formulas are more complex and are found in any operations management or management science textbook.

Beyond the formulas, operations managers must understand the psychology of waiting lines when considering how to staff the lines. Several innovations have helped waiting line management. The "snake" line, design most often found in amusement parks, is one example. Formerly, amusement park lines were straight and proceeded to infinity, often discouraging patrons from entering the queue. By bending the line with wooden or steel rails, the line becomes more compact and less psychologically forbidding. An occasional sign such as "45 minute wait from this point," helps the customer know what to expect.

Another example can be found at fast-food restaurants. The wireless headset found on the drive-through servers enables them to prepare food and talk at the same time, speeding the customer time through the queue.

David Maister (1985) outlined eight key propositions to the psychology of waiting.

1. Unoccupied time feels longer than occupied time. Some waiting line managers have alleviated boredom for customers standing in line by offering television sets, reading material, or educational material to occupy the customer's time.
2. Preprocess waits feel longer than in-process waits. A customer who is waiting to get a table in a restaurant (pre-process) feels more anxiety than the customer who has already been seated and is waiting for service (process).
3. Anxiety makes waits seem longer. Customers who are waiting for a purchase and perhaps uncertain if they will successfully gain admission or are in a hurry to get somewhere are in an increased sense of anxiety, and any wait at all is magnified by that anxiety.
4. Uncertain waits are longer than known, finite waits. When there is no certainty about the length of the wait, the customer's anxiety increases. An example is when a person gets stuck in a traffic jam and is not able to see the cause of the jam.
5. Unexplained waits are longer than explained waits. A person waiting for the mail will be less upset if the mail is delivered late during a torrential rain storm than on a clear, sunny day.

6. Unfair waits are longer than equitable waits. When I was in the U.S. Army, I twice witnessed fist fights caused by soldiers breaking into the "chow" line. If another customer is unfairly moved ahead of you in the queue, irritability makes the wait seem longer.
7. The more valuable the service, the longer the customer will wait. A customer is going to wait longer in line to buy tickets to a coveted concert than they will wait for an event they care little about.
8. Solo waits feel longer than group waits. Bring a friend to wait in line. If you don't, the time feels longer.

Customer satisfaction is directly related to their painless penetration of the waiting line. It is a critical element of service management. Expectations for waiting in line obviously differ internationally. It may take an hour to buy a McDonald's hamburger in Russia and no one is upset about it. If it took five minutes in the United States, people would balk at the system.

INTERNATIONALIZING SERVICES

The growth of international trade in services is a natural outgrowth of a highly productive industrial economy. Services become an important part of the nation's economy and account for a majority of the nation's employment in developed countries. Cross-the-border trade in service by 10 major countries belonging to the Organization for Economic Cooperation and Developments (OECD) (the United States, Japan, the United Kingdom, the Federal Republic of Germany, France, Italy, Canada, the Netherlands, Spain, and Switzerland) increased from $120 billion in 1975 to $253 billion in 1985 (Gonenc, 1988). The bulk of the international trade in services takes place inside the OECD countries, among which the United States, Japan, the United Kingdom, and Germany are the major service export countries. Two types of services are often traded internationally, according to Gonenc (1988). The first type is the supply of capital and labor resources serving as the infrastructure to other international activities. Examples include international transportation, communications, finance, and insurance. This type of service is the most dominant form of international trade in services. The second type comprises services such as engineering, consultancy, computer services, and accounting services that are traded internationally because of some kind of monopoly, a proprietary service, or a cost advantage.

There are two types of services that are not commonly traded internationally or have a limited international competition. Services such as railway transportation, electricity distribution, and water services and health, education, and retirement insurance are highly regulated by government and usually exempt from foreign competition. Foreign competition is severely limited in services whose needs and demands are structured by local business and bounded by local culture, and thus can be satisfied by hardly anyone except local, long-established service suppliers. Services with high international transaction costs are also traded to a very limited extent.

International involvement in services usually takes three forms. The first form involves exporting services that minimize the firm's investment and control in foreign markets. This type of service often requires low customer involvement, embodies more physical elements, and is easy to be exported.

The second type consists of services sold to foreign markets through licensing, franchising, and contractual agreement. Services such as management know-how, marketing knowledge, retailing, and fast-food chains are a few examples. Service firms have more investment, control, involvement in foreign markets. This type of services usually involves people, knowledge, technology, skills, and physical goods.

Maximum investment, control, and involvement in foreign markets can be achieved through direct investment such as the establishment of branches, wholly-owned subsidiaries, and mergers and acquisitions. Consulting, accounting, and advertising services that have high customer involvement in service production and delivery processes and require a considerable degree of localization are good candidates for foreign direct investment.

Service managers who move outside of their home country must keep two principles in mind:

1. Adapt to the local employee customs.
2. Adapt to the local customers.

If an entire culture is accustomed to taking a siesta at noon, then the local American Express employees must do the same. Companies that do not attempt to adapt are viewed as outsiders by local communities, and that can be threatening to one's survival if political turmoil erupts in a foreign land.

Adapting to the tastes of local customers may be primarily a marketing function, however, the expectations of local customers play heavily into the operations management of the firm. Such elements as sourcing, service quality, staffing, productivity measurements, and distribution are effected by variations in international customer tastes.

REFERENCES

Albrecht, K. and R. Zemke (1985). *Service America: Doing Business in the New Economy*. Homewood, IL: Dow Jones-Irwin.

Barras, R. (1986). "Towards a Theory of Innovation in Services." *Research Policy*, 15:161–173.

Chase, Richard B. (1981). "The Customer Contact Approach to Services: Theoretical Bases and Practical Extension." *Operations Research*, 29(4): 698706.

Collier, D. A. (1983). "The Service Sector Revolution: The Automation of Services." *Long Range Planning*, 16(6):10–20.

Daniels, P. W. (1993). *Service Industries in the World Economy*. Oxford, United Kingdom: Blackwell.

Davidow, W. H. and B. Uttal. (1989). "Service Companies: Focus or Falter." *Harvard Business Review*, Vol. 6: 77–85.

Elfring, T. (1989). "New Evidence on the Expansion of Service Employment in Advanced Economies." *The Service Industries Journal*, 9:337–356.

Fimstahl, T. W. (1989). "My Employees Are My Service Guarantee." *Harvard Business Review*, Vol. 66: 28–32.

Gonenc, R. (1988). "Changing Economics of International Trade in Services," in B. R. Guile and J. B. Quinn (eds.), *Technology in Services*. Washington, DC: National Academy Press, pp. 167–186.

Hart, C. W. L., J. L. Heskett, and W. E. Sasser, Jr. (1990). "The Profitable Art of Service Recovery." *Harvard Business Review*, Vol. 68: 148–156.

Hart, C. W. L. (1988). "The Power of Unconditional Service Guarantees." *Harvard Business Review*, Vol. 66: 54–62.

Maister, D. (1985). "The Psychology of Waiting Lines," in J. A. Czepiel, M. R. Solomon, and C. F. Surprenant (eds). *The Service Encounter*. Lexington, MA: Lexington Books, D.C. Heath and Company.

Quinn, J. B. (1988). "Technology in Services: Past Myths and Future Challenges," in B.R. Guile and J.B. Quinn (eds.), *Technology in Services*. Washington, DC: National Academy Press, pp. 16–46.

Quinn, J. B. (1992). *Intelligent Enterprises*. New York: The Free Press.

Reichheld, F. F. and W. E. Sasser, Jr. (1990). "Zero Defections: Quality Comes to Services." *Harvard Business Review*, Vol. 68:105–111.

Schmenner, R. W. (1993). *Production/Operations Management* (3rd ed.). New York: Macmillan Publishing Co.

Zeithaml, V. A., A. Parasuraman, and L. L. Berry (1990). *Delivering Quality Service*. New York: The Free Press.

12

Coordination

Scott T. Young and Caron St. John

Managing global networks of people, plants, and supplies requires expert coordination among the business functions, including operations, marketing, accounting, research and development, finance, customer service, human resources, and information systems.

Porter (1986) identified the specific problem of coordinated functional decision-making: "In each functional area of a firm, whether it be finance, marketing, production, or R&D, the need to coordinate activities in different countries has become imperative. . . . Different activities within the firm are located in different countries, raising the complexity of the coordination task. . . . Those firms that exploit their international networks through coordinating across countries are turning out to be the winners" (pg. 6).

Marketing and manufacturing are most responsible for the interface between product and customer; therefore, the coordination of these two functions has a substantial impact on the continued survival of the firm. The tenuous marketing-manufacturing relationship of the global organization is aggravated by complex structural, geographic, and cultural considerations that give the coordination task an added dimension of complexity.

In this chapter, we are concerned with the structuring and coordination issues that influence the operations relationship with other functions during the implementation of international strategies.

INTERNATIONAL STRATEGY IMPLEMENTATION

Strategies, international and domestic, are implemented through the pattern of day-to-day decisions made and actions taken over time. For an organization's strategy to be implemented as planned, marketing and manufacturing must make decisions and take actions that are consistent with the strategy of the firm and with each other. Coordination between marketing and manufacturing is critical because of the extreme interdependency that exists between the two groups. Thompson (1967) described the form of interdependency that exists between marketing and manufacturing as reciprocal interdependency, with manufacturing providing outputs (products) that marketing must have to accomplish its objectives and marketing providing outputs (product and market requirements) that manufacturing must have to accomplish its objectives. The two groups are interdependent in their daily activities associated with production schedules and handling of special customer requests. They are also interdependent in their long-range decisions about new product introductions, capacity planning, and cost versus differentiation competitive priorities.

Many organizations discover an adversarial relationship between marketing and manufacturing. Each group, in the absence of strong organizational guidance, tends to subscribe to goals that further the performance of the department at the expense of the total organization.

Marketing tends to pull the organization toward higher levels of market differentiation, whereas manufacturing tends to pull the organization toward a higher degree of standardization and scale economies. Shapiro (1977) argued that the areas where marketing-manufacturing coordination is most needed but most susceptible to parochial points of view are capacity planning and long range sales forecasting, production scheduling and short-range sales forecasting, inventory levels and delivery capabilities, quality standards and control performance, breadth of product line, focus and implications of cost-control efforts, and the need for and frequency of new product introductions.

One of the reasons marketing and manufacturing groups fail to see the interdependence that exists between them is that their daily activities are so disparate. It is because their activities are so different that they are typically grouped into separate departments with independent organization hierarchies that merge at the top levels of the organization. Tjosvold (1989) argued that employees use the organization's structure when concluding their goals are interdependent, and if so, whether the interdependence is competitive or collaborative. The separation of marketing and manufacturing in the organization structure signals to employees that the goals of the two departments are either not interdependent at all, or if interdependence exists, it is competitive rather than collaborative. For the international organization, the problem of creating an environment of collaborative interdependency is particularly difficult since the traditional problems of parochial competitive attitudes derived from the organization structure may be further aggravated by distance and culture.

Structuring Issues

The managerial process of strategy implementation is concerned with the development of organization structures and coordination methods to ensure that the pattern of strategy created over time is consistent with the organization's planned strategy. The first issue in implementing strategy is the design of organization structure. The structuring problem in strategy implementation may be addressed at two levels: the primary level and the operating level (Hrebiniak and Joyce, 1984). Primary level structure describes the relationship among the major operating units of the entire organization and reflects the diversity of businesses in which the firm participates. For the international firm, primary level structuring decisions are concerned with the headquarters-subsidiary relationship and use of a centralized international divisional structure or a decentralized multinational form. As Garnier (1984) has noted, in the structuring of the international organization, the parent is torn by the internal pressures to centralize important decisions and external market pressures to decentralize.

Operating level structure outlines the arrangement of tasks and processes within the units of the primary structure, such as the departments within a unit or division (Hrebiniak and Joyce, 1984). The concerns when establishing operating structure are how to form and then coordinate interdependent departments so that the pattern of decisions made by these groups over time is consistent with the firm's formulated strategy. As with primary structure, operating structure (departments) should reflect the firm's strategy. The operating structure decisions that design the relationship between marketing and manufacturing are dictated by the firm's strategy and the constraining primary structure decisions.

Coordination Mechanisms

A second critical issue in the implementation of strategy is the development of mechanisms for coordinating among individuals and departments. While structural arrangements establish the formal lines of

Strategy Environment, Structural Decisions, and Coordinating Complexity

Strategy Environment   Structural Decisions   Coordinating Complexity

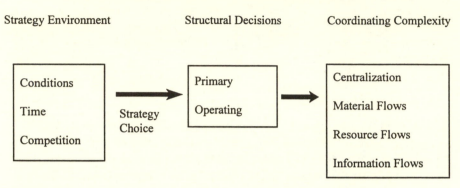

Figure 12-1

communication and authority, coordinating and control mechanisms ensure the proper implementation of daily decisions and activities. A contingency view pervades much of the work on coordinating mechanisms: environmental conditions and the firm's own strategy-structure choices determine the complexity of the coordination task. The chosen system of coordinating mechanisms should then reflect that complexity (see Figure 12–1).

Much of the work on interdepartmental coordinating mechanisms is derived from Lawrence and Lorsch's (1967) study of high-performance firms in different industry environments.

Lawrence and Lorsch concluded that successful firms used different kinds of interdepartmental integrating devices—depending on the competitive requirements in their industries. In those industries with high levels of change or turbulence, the coordination task was more difficult and required more complex methods of coordination. Galbraith (1973) advanced the findings of Lawrence and Lorsch by creating a hierarchy of mechanisms for integrating departments including centralization of decisions, decision rules, goal-setting and planning processes, direct contact and meetings, interdepartmental liaison roles, temporary task forces, permanent teams, integrating roles, and integrating departments. Galbraith maintained that each step down the list represented a more complicated mechanism of coordination and that the more complicated mechanisms were needed in more demanding environments. Rather than give up a lower level coordinating mechanism when coordination complexity increased, Galbraith argued that firms will add the next higher level of coordinating mechanism to their overall system of coordination.

STRATEGY, STRUCTURE, AND COORDINATION IN INTERNATIONAL BUSINESS

Herbert (1984) described several strategies that require a form of international organization structure. The first, most simple strategy is to export existing domestically produced products, with an organization goal of increased revenues. In this form of volume expansion strategy, slight modification of the operating level structure is required, with little or no change in primary structure. Typically, export sales and foreign market development responsibilities are housed in a staff department at corporate headquarters, with marketing representatives assigned to remote locations. The structure and reporting relationships of manufacturing operations would not be affected by the decision to export products.

In a volume expansion strategy, materials would follow a predictable, one-way flow from domestic production to domestic and international customers. Since all of production management and all of marketing senior management would be physically located domestically, managerial flows such as plans, schedules, and policies would be created in the domestic organization and provided to the foreign sales organizations. Strategic resources such as funds and personnel would be provided to the foreign offices when decisions were made by the home office to expand existing or develop new markets. The resource allocation decision would be driven by the availability of domestic production capacity. In general, the decision environment would be predictable and centrally controlled.

In many organizations pursuing a volume expansion strategy, there would be no increase in the difficulty of coordinating between marketing and manufacturing. Except for some front-end modification of packing and shipping materials, manufacturing would treat foreign and domestic orders alike. Orders for foreign customers would be handled through the same order placement and production scheduling systems as domestic orders. The nationality of the foreign customer would be invisible to production.

Success of the volume expansion strategy may bring about constrained production resources. If production resources are constrained in a firm pursuing a volume-enhancing strategy, there will be inadequate capacity to meet customer demand. Marketing and manufacturing coordination problems would likely center around the priority of domestic versus foreign customers, the integrity of production schedules, and handling of special requests (changes in due dates or order quantities). These types of routine issues that are common between marketing and manufacturing would likely be handled by increased efforts to develop valid market forecasts linked via computer to production schedules, production schedules that have valid due dates, as well as firm guidelines on the priorities of different customers and the circumstances for changing due dates and quantities in the production schedule.

Resource Acquisition

The second strategy/structure type described by Herbert is "resource acquisition." Under this type of strategy, the firm is importing low-cost or scarce resources for use in domestically manufactured and distributed goods. The resource acquisition strategy would usually require foreign production operations with minimal management structure, little staff support, and centralized decision-making conducted at the home office. Primary structure would not be modified, but operating structure changes would be required to establish the reporting linkage between foreign and domestic production facilities. These minor operating structure modifications would take place within the manufacturing organization and would, therefore, be invisible to marketing.

As with the volume expansion strategy, the resource acquisition strategy involves predictable, one-way material flows from the foreign production operations to the domestic operations. Finished goods are then shipped to customers. Creative/technical flows between domestic and foreign production would take the form of learning transferred from parent to foreign subsidiary. These technical flows would most likely be managed through the temporary assignment of technical personnel from the home office.

Since the management hierarchy is located domestically and the foreign production capability is a form of backward integration, further investment in the foreign organization would be a function of the justified cost-savings. Communications would tend to be directives from the home office to the subsidiary, with plans, policies, and schedules developed domestically. In general, the decision environment would be predictable and centrally controlled.

For marketing and manufacturing, coordination complexity would not increase under most circumstances. A resource acquisition strategy is a form of backward integration that has the potential to reduce the flexibility of the organization if the industry undergoes dramatic change. Since the intention of the strategy is to stabilize the company's position in its current business through improved supply access or reduced materials cost, pressures by marketing to differentiate the product line might meet resistance. If the environment is stable and the current strategy and raw material postures are good ones, then there would be no new coordination problems. However, if the environment is turbulent with pressures to modify products and broaden the product line, the fixed investment in existing supplies may hamper manufacturing's willingness to cooperate with marketing requests. In such a case, effective use of strategic planning techniques involving members from marketing and manufacturing would be needed to clarify the organization's position on low-cost versus differentiation strategies, the direction and extent of product development activities, and the speed with which organization transitions would be carried out.

Multidomestic/Integration

A third strategy/structure type described by Herbert is "integration." Herbert's international or integrated strategy type closely resembles Porter's (1986) description of the multidomestic industry where "the competitive advantages of the firm, then, are largely specific to the country." (p. 18) Under this multidomestic strategy, foreign and domestic markets are treated independently and equally, and each markets' needs and unique character determine the way products are developed and provided. International headquarters would provide strategic guidance and, possibly, centralized research and development. Autonomous national or regional divisions would manage product and market development, as well as production activities. In multidomestic industries, organizational units within firms may be operated independently using portfolio-like management techniques.

For a firm pursuing a multidomestic strategy, the strategic focus of the business is on national flexibility and responsiveness. The primary structuring decisions would separate organization resources into decentralized national or regional units. Within a national unit or division, the organization would likely be structured along functional lines, with marketing and manufacturing reporting to the national headquarters. The appearance of the operating structure would be similar to that of a domestic business. Except for broad policies and guidelines provided by the domestic headquarters, physical and managerial flows would take place within a national business unit. The creative/technical flows would consist of basic R&D transferred from headquarters to business units through formal technical reports and review sessions. Strategic resources would be allocated to national business units participating in attractive market segments.

In the multidomestic environment, the types of activities that create turbulence in the marketing-manufacturing relationship—new product introductions, changes to product specifications, unique market demands, and disruptions of production schedules—would all be handled within the individual national businesses. Under most circumstances, the marketing-manufacturing coordination problems would be the traditional ones observed in domestic businesses with no additional complications imposed by the nature of the international strategy. The multidomestic structure would create unique marketing-manufacturing coordination problems only if industry conditions changed so that complete independence was no longer desirable and competitive success was contingent on exchange linkages between business units in two or more nations. In this type of environment, the primary coordination problem would be intrafunctional. Marketing in one national business would need to coordinate with marketing in another national business for transfer of market and product knowledge. Manufacturing departments from different national businesses would have to coordinate to exchange technical and process information. The need for information exchange (but not resource exchange) would likely require that marketing and manufacturing participate in task forces and committees to facilitate technology transfer and sharing of market information.

Early Global/Reciprocal

A fourth international strategy/structure type described by Herbert is "reciprocity." In this type of strategy, a firm might import raw materials or subcomponents, complete processing or final assembly in the domestic nation, and then ship the completed product out of the country for sale to export markets. In this type of strategy, production capacity is concentrated in a few plants to achieve economies of scale, products are standardized for worldwide commodity markets, and decision-making is centralized. This type of strategy requires a much higher level of coordination within the organization than any of the strategies described previously. Production schedules, delivery arrangements, and capacity balancing are further complicated by long shipping lead times and national/cultural boundaries.

This strategy type requires unique primary and operating structural changes. According to Herbert, a firm pursuing a reciprocity or early global strategy will likely develop an international division organized by geographical market segments, product lines, or functions. While marketing and manufacturing activities will take place in foreign nations, the two groups would be organizationally separate until the top levels of the international division. The structure would serve to buffer the technical core from various national and cultural forces. The coordinating environment would be characterized by complex but predictable flows. Physical materials would flow in from one country and out to others, crossing distance and national boundaries and complicating the purchasing, scheduling, and delivery tasks. Although the network of flows might be complex, it would be predictable and relatively constant over time. Technical information flows would include the sharing of cost-savings technology across production operations.

While cultural differences and distance would make coordination between marketing and manufacturing more difficult than in a domestic or multidomestic business, the relationship would not be characterized by frequent change. Because of the focus on standardized products, the international division would not be required to be responsive to the unique needs of national markets. The marketing groups would be responsible for identifying markets and adapting advertising and product placement strategies to local cultural conditions but those concerns would not result in product modifications that would interfere with production stability and scale economies. The organization would be structured for stability, centralized control, and efficiency rather than market flexibility. The relationships between foreign and domestic operations and between marketing and manufacturing groups, would be interdependent but stable. In this environment, information as well as physical resources are exchanged across national boundaries, but the type of information exchange would be technical and understandable to organization members regardless of nation of origin.

In this type of situation, typical sources of marketing and manufacturing conflict would be the integrity of production schedules and quality standards, scheduling priorities for customers, and capacity expansion (reduction) and balancing issues. Although foreign nationals would be employed in various marketing and manufacturing managerial positions, the centralized control structure would reduce uncertainty about strategies and competitive priorities. Coordinating mechanisms would most likely be associated with eliminating uncertainty and standardizing decisions through decision rules, procedure development, and hiring, promotion, and training programs that emphasized and rewarded behaviors that were consistent with the focus on standardized products and global economies. Coordinating mechanisms would also include systematic market research used to derive valid forecasts, and sophisticated production planning and scheduling systems that allow the firm to exploit production economies of scale while making on-time deliveries.

COMPLEX GLOBAL

In global industries, what Martinez and Jarillo (1989) call "complex global" businesses, a firm's competitive position in one country affects and is affected by its position in other countries. The extremes of autonomous, portfolio-like management (multidomestic) or centralized standardized production designed to exploit economies of scale (early global) will undermine competitive advantage and opportunities for world-wide integration. With a complex global strategy, it is common for raw materials to be purchased in the global marketplace, manufacturing plants to be located throughout the world to serve regional markets, world-wide manufacturing share to be a major determinant of product costs, while at the same time, products are developed and marketed to national and regional markets.

Bartlett and Ghoshal (1989) describe the organization form necessary for complex global industries as the transnational, the fifth international strategy/structure form discussed here. According to Bartlett and Ghoshal, traditional international structures provide two organizational alternatives: dependence and independence. Using the strategies previously described as examples, the foreign operations associated with the volume expansion and resource acquisition strategies are completely dependent on the domestic home office for policies, decisions, and resources. In the multidomestic structure, all foreign and domestic operations are independent of each other. Bartlett and Ghoshal propose that completely independent or dependent organizational forms are inappropriate for complex global competitive environments. They propose that complex interdependence—collaborative information-sharing, problem-solving, and resource-sharing—is required in global environments so that scale-efficient operations may be integrated, marketing knowledge exchanged, and financial resources used to cross-subsidize markets.

The major difference between the reciprocal/early global strategy and the complex global strategy is in the stability of the organization structure and predictability of the coordination requirements. The early global/reciprocal strategy, with its international divisional structure and competitive focus on global cost economies, would be stable over time. It would not be characterized by the type of conditions that require complex integrated organizational responses: frequent new product requirements, unique market demands, and reallocations of product and process requirements that alter cost economies. On the other hand, the complex global strategy and the transnational structure would be characterized by frequent primary and operating level structural changes and attempts to achieve simultaneous market flexibility and cost economies.

At the primary level of the transnational form, there would be no distinction between domestic and international segments of the business. The primary structure would be configured by products, markets, or processes—whichever was most appropriate for the organization at a given point in time. At the operating level, product-market teams would represent a limited line of products to a limited group of customers. The product-market teams would have representatives from marketing, manufacturing, and product development. In those types of business where economies of scale are necessary, the team members would serve as liaisons between customers and centralized manufacturing. In businesses where centralized production is not an advantage, but centralized R&D is, then team members would serve as the liaison between customers and R&D but would operate their own production facilities. The overall structure of the organization would not appear symmetrical. Product-market teams in some parts of the world would conduct their own applied product development, other teams would control their own production capacity. Physical materials would follow convoluted, ever-changing paths through the organization as common production lots are run to service multiple markets.

The transnational form would involve physical material flows, resources flows, and technical and social information flows within and between teams and between teams and their divisional or unit management. The objective in organization design would be to create the structure that best suited the cost and flexibility requirements for the local market opportunity. The high degree of decentralization would force the unit of analysis for strategic planning and resource allocations down to the team level. Teams would report into the organization through matrix-like arrangements with staff experts and specialists serving to coordinate teams.

In this type of environment, marketing and manufacturing activities are represented within teams. Since the structural barrier to cooperation is eliminated and, in many cases, the geographical and cultural barriers would be reduced because of the localized team structure, marketing-manufacturing coordination difficulties within teams would be expected to be low. In this final stage, instead of marketing and manufacturing competing with each other, the competition will be directed toward other teams. Team structure will communicate the importance of teamwork, cooperation and collaboration within teams, but it will accentuate differences with other parts of organization. It will encourage competition for scarce strategic resources: funds, production capacity, engineering specialists, and qualified team members. This type of competition will be very negative for the organization because cooperative resource and information sharing may be required for survival.

A second coordination difficulty would be hierarchical coordination between teams and the organization. There is a danger of frenetic, directionless, opportunistic movement by teams as they search for new opportunities.

Mechanisms for coordinating between teams and the organization would include staff generalists to serve as liaisons, and integrators to pull the specialist teams together. In addition to teams and liaison roles, use of formal strategic planning processes will be extensive, as will socialization activities to develop a common vision.

MARKETING-MANUFACTURING COORDINATION

The popular management literature claims that close manufacturing and marketing coordination is desirable. Hayes, Wheelwright, and Clark (1989) called this "the importance of adopting a holistic perspective," and they pointed out that the decision of one function interrelates and reinforces the decisions of another function.

Yet, anecdotal evidence persists that coordination problems between marketing and manufacturing continue to plague modern firms. Shapiro listed the areas in most need of coordination, including forecasting, inventory standards, quality standards, and cost-control efforts. Perhaps this is a natural result of the great disparity between the activities of manufacturing and marketing managers. This may be a unique problem to the United States due to the emphasis on functional specialization.

Given the need for close coordination between manufacturing and marketing, a set of coordination mechanisms must be suggested to accomplish this feat. The global organization increases the complexity between these functions even further. The global structure, the nature of cross-boundary flows, the state of collaboration between marketing and manufacturing (collaborative versus competitive), and cross-cultural complications are the key themes in determining appropriate coordination mechanisms. The choice of mechanisms is therefore situational and complex global strategies call for increasingly complex mechanisms, as suggested by Galbraith. The recent transition from interdepartmental to intradepartmental to interteam decision-making structures brings a new set of coordination considerations.

Because marketing and manufacturing is a unique coordination situation that encompasses the all-important customer interface, it is perhaps *the* critical issue in all organizational coordination decisions.

Operations and Research and Development

The central issue in coordinated decision-making between operations and research and development (R & D) is involvement. The design of new products or services must have operations management involvement to help assure a successful product implementation. New products/services are usually conceived by either the marketing or R & D department. Many times new product development passes to the "proceed to manufacture" stage before operations is aware of the new product.

Operations involvement in new product conception eases much of the uncertainties and difficulties that may arise in production. How to best manufacture a product should be addressed shortly after a proto-type is approved.

Service organizations are no different from manufacturing in the difficulties arising from the operations/R & D interface. Any new bank or airline product has an impact on operations scheduling, layout, and inventory planning and the absence of operations input can kill a new service introduction.

The concept of the team, "designing for manufacturability," is based on the early involvement of operations and customers in product de-sign. DFM teams succeed because of the involvement of several import-ant constituencies. Without operations involvement, serious design flaws may go undetected. Without customer involvement, a firm may release a product nobody wants. Without marketing involvement, com-petitive products may be fatally ignored.

Operations and Accounting

The biggest complaint about accounting in the 1980s was that it lacked a strategic vision in decision-making. Capital equipment pur-chases were vetoed because they didn't meet a predetermined rate of return. Faced with opportunities for new technologies that offer pro-ductivity and quality gains, operations managers not only must address the question, "Is it cost effective?" but also must answer the important question "What will happen if we don't go into this technology and our competition does?" That is the strategic area of operations that can be adversely impacted by a straightforward cost-benefit analysis.

Accounting, as a function, can support successful operations by de-livering pertinent information. Operations can support accounting by diligently striving for accuracy in record-keeping and following stan-dard accounting procedures.

CONCLUSIONS

The tendency to direct young managers in a straight-line career path into one specific functional area of the firm is the greatest deterrent to an overall understanding of organizational coordination. Modern man-agement thinking encourages job enlargement and flexibility for the line worker, with the belief that an increased variety of tasks makes the work more interesting. Yet many organizations do not apply this philosophy to the development of their managers. A good practice may be to cycle new managers for two years in accounting, two years in operations, and two years in marketing. The negative aspect to this practice is that much time and training might be wasted on an employee that leaves the company before the development cycle plays out. The advantage to this practice is that over the years, the organization develops a cadre of managers who are totally multidisciplined and the firm can better relate one activity to another.

Operations managers often suffer from this very weakness—they have a narrow view of the firm and are protectionist towards their production activities. Their major concerns are to meet production and delivery schedules and minimize inventory investment. Marketing requests for customer expedition are viewed with displeasure, and sometimes marketing does make promises that are impossible to deliver. It is imperative, however, that operations not become so removed from the customer that they fail to see the connection between the customer and the firm's survival. Manufacturing firms do not exist merely to keep machines running, and product flowing. Therefore, periodic visits by operations managers to the end-users of the product and escorted customer plant tours are critical activities for operations managers.

The operations manager must realize the holistic nature of the firm, and understand operations' role within that holistic system. The holistic relationship among functions often gets lost in the personal power struggles of corporate gamesmanship. Managers whose major focus becomes how to raise their income to afford a new house, a new boat, or membership in the country club may make decisions that compromise other areas of the company and upset the balance necessary to achieve success.

REFERENCES

Bartlett, C. A. and S. Ghoshal (1989). *Managing Across Borders: The Transnational Solution*. Boston: Harvard Business School Press.

Galbraith, J. R. (1973). *Designing Complex Organizations*. Reading, MA: Addison-Wesley.

Garnier, G. (1984). The Autonomy of Foreign Subsidiaries: Environmental and National Influences. *Journal of General Management*, 10(1):57–82.

Hayes, R. H., S. C. Wheelwright, and K. B. Clark (1988). *Dynamic Manufacturing*. New York: The Free Press.

Herbert, T. T. (1984). Strategy and Multinational Organization Structure: An Interorganizational Relationships Perspective. *Academy of Management Review*, 9(92):259–270.

Hrebiniak, L. G. and W. F. Joyce (1984). *Implementing Strategy*. New York: Macmillan.

Lawrence, P. R. and J. W. Lorsch (1967). *Organization and Environment*. Boston, MA: Harvard University Graduate School of Business Administration.

Martinez, J. T. and J. C. Jarillo (1989). The Evolution of Research on Coordination Mechanisms in Multinational Corporations. *Journal of International Business Studies*. Fall, 489–514.

Porter, M. E. (1986). *Competition in Global Industries*. Boston, MA: Free Press.

Shapiro, B. P. (1977). Can Marketing and Manufacturing Coexist? *Harvard Business Review*. Vol. 55:104–114, Reprint No. 77511.

Thompson, J. P. (1967). *Organizations in Action*. New York: McGraw-Hill.

Tsjovold, D. (1989). Cooperative and Competitive Interdependence. *Group and Organization Studies*, 13 (3):275–289.

13

Human-Centered Production

This chapter introduces a concept called human-centered production (HCP). Given the changing state of organizational forms, and the re-emphasis on teams as a management force, it is time to reawaken the need for managers to go one-on-one with their employees, and for fellow team members to appreciate and tolerate individual differences. Human-centered production requires an understanding of individuality and uniqueness.

Organizations of the 1990s are experimenting with different ways to structure working relationships. Global operations managers must configure their organizations so that they perform effectively. Global business forces managers to constantly change the way they operate, and empowered teams are one of the current approaches to modern management. In this chapter, new organizational forms and accompanying team issues are reviewed as a prelude to HCP.

NEW ORGANIZATIONAL FORMS

Tom Peters and Robert Waterman associated lean organizational structures with management excellence in their book, *In Search of Excellence* (1982). They noted that organizations bloated with unnecessary layers of management increasingly faltered under the weight of bureaucracy.

Since the publication of Peters and Waterman's book, many organizations have struggled to cut as many layers as possible. Anecdotes abound of successful restructures. A number of authors have proposed intriguing ideas on how best to structure the organizations of the 21st century. Two of these authors are Charles Handy and James Brian Quinn.

Handy's Organizations

Management theorist Charles Handy discussed three new forms of organization in his book, *The Age of Unreason* (1989). The "shamrock" organization metaphorically represents three very different organizational groups in the form of a three-leafed shamrock. Handy pointed out that each group is "managed differently, paid differently, organized differently."

The professional core is one leaf, comprising of professionals, technicians, and managers. These are the highest paid members of the work force, should be the fewest in number, and are currently the most likely group to be reduced when organizations downsize.

The second leaf consists of outside organizations contracted to accommodate the production and delivery process: subcontractors, consultants, brokers, and retailers. This leaf is responsible for many important aspects of production. Although they receive paychecks from a different employer, individuals in these firms are often critical to the success of the organizations they serve.

The third leaf is the flexible labor force: the temporary and part-time workers who are not paid full benefits. These workers are also indispensable, if not permanent. Handy wrote:

> Life in the core of more and more organizations is going to resemble that in consultancy firms, advertising agencies, and professional partnerships. The organizations are flat, seldom with more than four layers of rank, the top one being the assembly of partners, professionals, or directors. Promotion through the ranks comes quickly if you are any good (anyone of ability expects to be a partner before 40). Promotion, therefore, soon becomes an inadequate way of rewarding and recognizing people; success for those in the top rank can only mean doing the same job better and, presumably, for more money. At this level, therefore, much of the employee's pay is based on the results of the organization. The employee is in fact, if not in law, a partner. (p. 95)

Handy mentions a fourth leaf, the actual customer, who is sometimes put into the production system. Customers who pump their own gasoline, do bank transactions through automated teller machines, create their own salads, and bag their own groceries are members of this growing fourth leaf.

Handy emphasizes that the core is the essential hub—the "real" organization. Each leaf of the shamrock has different requirements and calls for different managerial considerations.

A second organizational form Handy discusses is "the federal organization."

> Federalism implies a variety of individual groups allied together under a common flag with some shared identity. Federalism seeks to make it big by keeping it small, or at least independent, combining autonomy with cooperation. It is the method which businesses are slowly, and painfully, evolving for getting the best of both worlds—the size which gives them clout in the marketplace and in the financial centers, as well as some economies of scale, and the small unit size which gives them the flexibility which they need, as well as the sense of community for which individuals increasingly hanker. (p. 117)

Handy is careful not to confuse federalism with decentralization. He points out that many organizations federalize without planning to—it is a reaction to the vast amounts of information needed to manage today's organizations. Organizations must make quick decisions, right or wrong, without asking for 45 authorities to anoint the decision.

Handy's third organizational type is the triple I organization. The formula for effectiveness is $I^3 = AV$. The three I's are intelligence, information, and ideas. These I's equal added value. It is what the management team knows and how they use it that equates with success.

James Brian Quinn discusses a number of new organizational forms in his book, *Intelligent Enterprise* (1992). Of these forms, the "spider's web" is one designed for situations in which autonomy is necessary. Central authority is reduced to a minimum. The center of the organization collects and transfers information from smaller organizational units. Quinn mentions investment banking, consulting, and technology development firms as examples of businesses that use spider's webs but notes that individual functions within a firm may employ this form. Spider's webs are especially appropriate for cross-functional teams.

> Here we find a very organic structure, little formalization of behavior, and numbers of highly specialized individuals working on an ad hoc basis toward a common interest. Why is this form so often used for innovation? To innovate means to break away from established patterns, to move rapidly and creatively in new realms; hence the most effective innovation groups often abandon the trappings of formal organizations and their planning and control systems. Interacting in a way that maximizes learning, potential knowledge gains, and progress through what are called "network externalities," if a number of individuals (n) work in parallel, but individually alone, on a project, their expected knowledge output would

be n times the output of one individual. If they share information and don't duplicate work, and if the information of each person is of importance to the others, the potential output relative to that of an individual should be approximate the function $2^{(n-1)}-1$. This is a powerful multiple, limited only by the capacity of individuals to absorb information.

Jessica Lipnack and Jeffrey Stamps (1993) called such structures "teamnets"—networks of teams that cross boundaries. Lipnap and Stamps expanded Quinn's spider's web organization to include multi-organizational alliances such as joint ventures, consortia, and flexible manufacturing networks. They listed five important principles to teamnets:

1. Unifying purpose
2. Independent members
3. Voluntary links
4. Multiple leaders
5. Interactive levels

Lipnack and Stamps disputed the need to flatten organizations.

> Appealing as the image of "flatness" is, especially in our bureaucracy-burdened society, it unfortunately is just plain wrong. Boundary crossing teamnets are lumpy, clustered, and multileveled forms of organization. People wear many hats and act at many levels. (p. 50)

Team-Centered Organizations

The popularity of teams in the organizations of the 1990s is not surprising, considering the success many companies have been reported. This popularity has been some time in coming. For many years, organizational theorists and organizational designers have praised the advantages of team-centered results over individual-centered results.

The jargon varies from "autonomous work groups" to "self-directed work groups" to "empowered teams," but the ideas are the same. Among the responsibilities of these teams are (Wellins, Byham and Wilson, p. 5):

Shared management and leadership
Planning
Controlling and improving work processes
Goal-setting
Self-inspection
Budget control and planning
Multiskilling

Training
Peer evaluation
Responsibility for quality

The famous sociotechnical studies in the British mining industry in the 1960s compared productivity and absenteeism after a group of miners applied autonomous work group principles. This group included multiskilling—group members were more cross-trained than the conventional group, the teams allocated tasks among themselves, payment of a bonus was allocated by the group in equal shares, and a high degree of autonomy was introduced. The conventional group continued to use the longwell method of mining, which was technology-dominated and highly specialized.

The results are given in Table 13–1.

The research in the impact of autonomous work groups on mining was led by Eric Trist and came under the heading of "sociotechnical systems theory." Trist's basic theory was that there was a best match between the technical environment and the social system.

The popular business press contains many stories of great results achieved through team-centered production. One longitudinal study in the 1970s attempted to study the effects of a team-building process. The research team (Kimberly and Nielsen, 1975, Pate, Nielsen, and Mowday, 1977) used questionnaires to measure the organizational climate and various output measures before and after a team-building training program. This study was carried out at an automobile assembly plant. The results are given in Table 13–2.

The results of this study clearly indicate an improvement of organizational climate. The researchers in the study team hesitated to attribute

Table 13–1

Comparisons of Autonomous Work Group to Conventional Method

	Conventional	Autonomous
Productivity as a percent of estimated face potential	78	95
Percent of shifts lagging behind established production cycle	69	5
Absenteeism without reason as a percent	4.3	.4
Absenteeism because of sickness as a percent	6.8	4.6

(Adapted from Eric L.Trist, G.W. Higgin, H. Murray, and A.B. Pollock. *Organizational Choice: Capabilities of Groups at the Coal Face under Changing Technologies*. London: Tavistock, 1963, pp. 123, 125.)

Table 13–2
Results of Team-Building Program

Measure	Before	After
Organizational Climate		
Trust	3.7	4.8
Support	3.8	4.4
Open communications -	3.0	4.6
Understanding of objectives	4.5	5.3
Commitment to objectives	4.4	5.2
Handling of conflict	3.8	4.9
Utilization of member resource	3.8	4.8
Self-direction	3.2	4.8
Supportive environment	3.2	4.6
Supervisory behavior		
Listening	3.5	4.5
Expressing ideas	4.1	5.1
Influence	2.9	4.1
Decision making	3.4	4.4
Relations with others	2.9	3.9
Task orientation	4.2	4.9
Handling of conflict	3.7	4.3
Willingness to change	4.3	5.0
Problem solving	3.3	4.3
Self-development	3.2	4.0
Production rates		
Number of cars per month	27,745	26,813
Percentage of acceptable quality cars	69	90
Profitability		
Monthly profit	-$116,995	19,983
Absenteeism		
Average percent absent	9.9	7.9

(Source: adapted from Kimberly, J.R. and W.R. Nielsen. "Organizational Development and Change in Organizational Performance," *Administrative Science Quarterly*, 20:196–201, 1975, and Pate, L.E., W.R. Nielsen, and R.T. Mowday. "A Longitudinal Assessment of the Impact of Organization Development on Absenteeism, Grievance Rates, and Product Quality," *Academy of Management Proceedings*, 1977, p. 354.)

the quality improvements to their team-building program due to coincidental engineering improvements. However, quality improvements should be expected, given the improvement in the organizational climate.

Wellins, Byham, and Wilson proposed a four-stage process for team design. The first stage involved having a vision of where the organization wanted to be. The second stage included making an assessment of the current versus the desired states of the organization, and creating a plan for getting to the desired state. The third stage was the actual implementation of teams. The fourth stage was the monitoring of the teams' effectiveness.

Organizational size is very much akin to human body fat. Elite organizations, like elite athletes, operate at such a high level of efficiency, that very little fat is found on the elite organization. As soon as the organization grows complacent and lazy, it begins to add fat. There is some minimal level of body fat with which firms best operate. To go below that level, firms risk not having enough energy to perform. Organizations, like human beings, can compete with higher levels of fat, but most likely will lose world-class status, unless all other organizations grow similarly fat.

The Turris Mine

The Turris Mine, a small coal mine in Elkhart, Illinois, is a modern-day example of the successful introduction of team concepts. Before each shift change, the miners are briefed about any problems or potential quality concerns. Then, the coal miners are guided through physical exercises designed to warm up their bodies for the difficult work ahead.

Individual performance evaluations are made by other team members. The miners do all of their own hiring. They work together in teams and respect most the managers who "go underground." These are the managers who actually come into the mine to talk to the miners about their work. Working in a mine is always a risky business, and the manager who comes down to where the work gets done gains the respect of the miners. It is analogous to the general who visits the troops in the fox hole. "Going underground" is a management concept that applies outside of mines, to all forms of work. Managers cannot afford to be removed from the work process.

At the invitation of David Dyches, the employee relations manager, we interviewed two miners and David to discover how the mine achieved the high level of job satisfaction it was noted for.

Theresa Allen, one of only five women coal miners at Turris, said:

> I've been at the mine eight years. I worked mostly in factories until I
> came here. I got laid off at Caterpillar for like a year and a half. I got

accepted to nursing school the same day I got hired at the mine. I needed the money more than I needed to spend the money for school, so I came to work here instead. I never thought I'd be a coal miner.

I work on conveyor belts. I keep them clean, do the maintenance on them. I have set steel, laid rail, secured falls. Everyone here does just about everything. There's no such thing as "that's not my job." If something needs doing, and you're there, everyone pitches in. Basically, I take care of belts, but if something else needed to be done, they needed the people, I'd go.

I was scared to death. I'd never been underground, I had no idea what it was going to be like. For about two days before I started, I was sick. I couldn't eat, I couldn't sleep. As soon as I got down there and saw what it was like, it didn't bother me. My grandfather was a coal miner but things were a lot different back in his days. I remember him talking about it. It never has bothered me, being underground. Some of the guys I started with couldn't handle it and they quit. They thought it was too confining. To me, it's not any more confining than working in a factory when you're walking between two rows of stacked-up boxes. Actually, it's better because you can't look out the window to see what a beautiful day it is and know what you're missing.

I work swing shifts. Right now I'm working 10–hour days and 10–hour nights and rotate every week. It's real dirty and dark, humid. It's about 50 to 60 degrees year-round. When you're working, you sweat and you have to take a sweatshirt or jacket because when you quit working, you get cold. You dress in layers. When you sit down and eat, there's no such thing as washing your hands. You just sit down on the dirt or a rock and eat your lunch. You get used to it. My niece came by one time to see me when I was just getting off. She looked at my clothes and couldn't believe how dirty I was. Everyone looks the same, so you don't worry about how dirty you are.

When my grandfather mined, it was all blasting and they shoveled by hand and mules pulled it out. Now it's all automated. But there's still a lot of shoveling. It's still hard work. There's not one job down there that's not hard, but I can't imagine doing it the way my grandfather did.

Sometimes you don't think you're going to make it, but you do. I'm sore now (*She has yet to start work*). I get up and can't hardly move. When I first started here, the first six weeks, I thought about buying stock in Ben-Gay. I couldn't move. But I'd been laid off for a year and a half and hadn't done anything, so I was really out of shape.

There's a lot of stuff that I can't do by myself, that I'm not strong enough. You just ask for help. The guys have to do that too. I used to do what I could by myself and I'd end up getting hurt, so now I don't hesitate to ask. They're real good to work with.

I've been off a couple times with my back when I was setting steel. That's a real heavy job. It still bothers me, but I can live with it. Luckily, I've never been injured seriously.

There are five women in the mine out of about 180. The first five years I worked here, I was the only woman. There's probably a few men underground who resent women. They don't have anything against me personally, it's just they're traditional and they don't think women should be working in a mine, let alone working at all. No one's ever said anything. Everybody down here's got family. You do a lot of talking when you're working, you learn a lot about each other and you make a lot of friends. You're real close because you're spending 10 hours a day with this person. Sometimes that's more than you spend with your family, so you learn a lot about each other.

What bothered me the most was the spitting. Almost everyone down there chews. That's something my mother wouldn't tolerate. It drove me crazy for a while, but it doesn't bother me any more. You get used to everything, I guess. I did carry some chew with me for a while. Just because the guys get so grumpy when they run out.

What I really like is about anything that you want to learn, they'll teach you. They put me through EMT (Emergency Medical Technician) training. That's something that I always wanted to do when I got the opportunity. About any class you're interested in, they'll get you in. Any different job or skill, they'll work with you. If you have personal problems, home problems and it's interfering with your work, they'll work with you.

It's the hardest job I've ever had, most physically demanding, but I like it better than any job I've had. Mainly, it's because the freedom they give you. They teach you how to do the work and then they tell you what they want done and where they want it done and you're on your own. You decide the best way you think, the safest way and they don't care if it takes longer as long as it's safe. Never have I heard of them giving trouble if a job took too long, as long as it was done safe and right. Before, I always worked in factories where you've got two foremen standing behind you watching you work or two foremen for every five people. Here, we have coordinators and managers, but they work right with you. The other day, we had a big spill and our managers, coordinators, maintenance people were all down there with shovels to help it get going again. As I said, there's no such thing as "This is not my job." This is the first place I've ever worked at that was like that. Everywhere else I've worked it was "That's not my category. That's not my job." People take a lot of pride in their work here. They give you a feeling of ownership. We take pride in the fact that we don't get any citations on our belts. We have very little downtime. We keep them clean. It's kind of like they give you a piece of ownership. Even though it's not yours, that part of it is your responsibility. You want to keep it looking good, because that reflects on you.

This is the first company I ever worked at where they really care about the people. If you're working for someone you know really cares, you do a better job for them. To some managers, you're just a number and they don't even know who you are. All of the doors are off here. If you want to come talk to the President, you just walk in and talk to him.

My superintendent, when I started he was in maintenance. Then he became a coordinator. Then he became a manager and now superintendent. But he's still just a worker, just like the rest of us. It's easier to talk to someone like that. It's easier to explain problems you're having with the equipment because they've done it, they've been down there and they understand. Whereas in some companies, a lot of them come right out of school into the office and have no idea what you're talking about. Almost everyone here has worked underground or they go underground regularly. They don't just sit in an office and do paperwork. The managers want to see what's going on.

I really don't think I could go back to a factory again. At Caterpillar, even your bosses didn't know your name. They just knew your check number and how many people they had. Here, everyone knows everyone. Because we're so small. Every year the President sends you a birthday card. I think that's kind of a nice gesture. Being the few women that there are here, I've never had any trouble, which is something I couldn't say at the factory. For some reason, underground, I think it's because you depend on each other so much. If you get hurt, you have to depend on the other person to help you. There are a lot of personalities that clash, but they try to take care of them. They'll just put them away from each other.

The only bad thing about being underground is the winter. When you're driving to work, it's dark. You work in the dark all day. By the time you get home in the evening, it's dark again. So the only time you see daylight is on your days off and it does get to be depressing. I spend more time outside now than ever.

Bob Pinkston, a maintenance miner:

My job right now is equipment maintenance, which involves working on all the equipment we have underground in the mine. We're responsible for repairing and getting back on-line as soon as possible.

Whenever I heard that they were going to build this mine, I was convinced that I was going to get hired on here. I went and got a mining degree at Wabash Valley College. I was about two thirds of the way through that when I got hired. I went on and finished an associate's degree in mining. I'm sure it helped me a lot.

You're expected to make decisions and be a key part in the way the mine's run. I like the responsibility that you have. I'm a coordinator in the maintenance department, which is the next level behind manager. The manager depends on the coordinator to pass on policy and day to day decisions. You have to set priorities about what to fix first and be able to react quick to emergencies that come up. You've got to be alert and on the ball.

When I first came down here, they took us on a tour. It was just amazing in the tunnels, everything black and equipment zooming around. It was just like stepping off a spaceship onto another planet. The first two weeks working here, it was troubling—the uncertainty of whether the rock's going to fall, learning how to operate the equipment, the dirt and filth. After a short period of time, you become accustomed to it.

You never know what dark is until you get into a tunnel and you're by yourself and you turn your light off. You can't see your hand in front of your face. It's like sticking your head in a bucket of tar and opening up your eyes. Our lamps have two filaments in the bulbs, so if one burns out, you've got a spare. Most people are smart, they check their bulbs and make sure they're both working. It is kind of spooky. My folks have a hard time figuring out why we don't have electrical lights all over.

Most of the equipment does the hard work for us. At first, the low top was what was terrible. The top is probably five feet tall. You're walking bent over, carrying about 12 pounds of weight. You bump your head all the time and my back was killing me. Then you get accustomed to it. The first weeks were the hardest.

My great-uncle retired from a mine. I visited him and told him about this modern way of mining and he couldn't comprehend the way we mine coal. In his days, it was by hand, with explosives and livestock. I never got any inspiration from him to go to work in a mine. The economy is what directed me over here. The wages were good, the benefits were good. Now that I'm in it, I can't imagine doing anything different. It's such a close knit group of people here. You know everybody from the President on down to the ladies that clean the building for us. You know them on a first name basis. It's not like going to work, it's a social gathering in a sense.

As far as management here on the mine, it's all personal, face to face. Management backs you 100 percent. If a person is concerned about their job, they'll get aggravated when things don't go right. Some people could care less. They just work their shift, go home and forget about it. Sometimes, you have to depend on other people to carry their end of the load and make everything work smooth. When they drop the ball, that's when I get frustrated.

The work ethic is strong in this area. Most of the people they hired are, number one, nonunion people, number two, inexperienced miners. What they had going for them was good rural backgrounds. Typically, you see more mature people, more dependable, with greater problem-solving skills working with equipment. They know what responsibility is. Most of the people they hired here had those qualities. They were able to learn and they took pride in where they worked. Therefore, they put out extra effort. The team concept that they have here, you don't want to be the weak link in the chain. They depend on peer pressure and self-pride. I think that's why this mine is so successful.

You can tell the college educated. The degreed people don't have much work experience. They come in, they're kind of hesitant to relate day-to-day activities with the people. They can talk and communicate amongst their peers, but there's a different level between some of them.

So you was David's professor? Did he tell you about the teasing that he got for using such big words? He'd get in these operations meetings and he was making a presentation and he said, "Caveat." Everyone said, "Whoa! Whoa! What the hell you talking about? What's the matter with you, using words like that?" They just rode him to death. Every time they'd see him out in the hall, they'd say, "Hey caveat!" Poor old Dave got embarrassed. He was going to have to learn about using top words they don't understand. They don't put up with that stuff. Of course, it's all good natured kidding. You might ask him how's his caveat's doing.

David Dyches, the employee relations supervisor:

Shell Mining recruits people, for the most part, from the Midwest, and they like people who worked their way through college and worked when they were younger. I grew up in Sanpete County, Utah. My grandma says that the only thing that grows there are kids. It's true. You have to really work to make a living down there. I think they liked that I worked with blue collar–type people. I came from a mining background. My great-grandfather and my grandfather were both coal miners when it was very dangerous. I hope they just didn't pick my name out of a hat.

The technicians are not the only ones who are multiskilled. My boss just moved from manager of employee relations to Midwest manager of coal sales. So he went from employee relations to marketing. I kind of run the gamut. I've been exposed to labor issues, the EEO stuff, Affirmative Action, sexual harassment. My real job is a kind of consultant to the supervisors. For the most part, they've worked their way up from the technician and supervisory level and haven't had an exposure to legal issues and dealing with people. I help them be better managers. We do payroll, benefits administration, American Disabilities Act. When you hear Employee Relations, that's pretty much what it is—pay, benefits, performance evaluations.

One of the things that is most significant as far as showing that everyone's equal: there's only one door and no reserved parking spots at the coal mine. The President doesn't have his own spot or a paid-for car.

It starts right from hiring. Every person is expected to take an aptitude test and I barely passed it. I would have barely been considered as a technician. I consider myself reasonably intelligent and the tests are tough. The employees, the technicians, do the interviewing. They'll pair up with the supervisor and interview applicants. So you're interviewed by your peers. It works well. No one can complain about your coworkers when it's you that hired them. Another good thing is the information sharing. The good news is that we've improved our cost per ton every year we've been in operation, but the bad news is our price per ton has gone down more. We're still losing money and the organization is willing to share that sort of detailed financial data with the employees. The employees are mature enough to understand and want to learn. They always want more information and you wonder how far you go without your competitors knowing everything about your business. They are information starved. How is business? What are the costs like?

The mine is 10 years old. I don't know how the culture developed, but I think through the things we talked about of hiring good people and getting them involved. There isn't a decision made at the mine that the employees don't have input on.

I'm dependent upon them underground and I think they feel dependent upon me above ground, to make sure they get paid. It's not their environment in my office. They have a much more difficult time talking about concerns with manager or coworkers or pay and equity issues. When you're underground, they'll give it to you with both barrels. So I try to get down there as much as possible. Although my great grandma really opposes it. Her husband died of black-lung. He started out working in southern Illinois and emigrated to Price, Utah. He told her all the horror stories. When she found out I was going to work for a coal mine, she didn't like that at all. In the early 1900s there were 20,000 deaths a year in mining and now there are 50 or 60.

THE INDIVIDUAL'S PLACE IN HUMAN-CENTERED PRODUCTION

If team-centered production is to succeed, human-centered production must be practiced. Human-centered production is a production system that relies on the synergistic effect of a group of individuals to make quality products and provide quality service. A human-centered production system contains a group of individuals whose intention is to do good work.

The value and uniqueness of the individual must not be lost within the team-centered approach. After all, a team *is* a collection of people who have differing motivations and wants. A starting point for creating a human-centered approach is simply to get managers to recognize the importance of the job to each individual. Many times, workers become anonymous faces without human histories. It is imperative that managers know their work force. They do not have to be friends with them, but they should respect them and attempt to understand what makes them tick. The quiz in Table 13–3 (next page) might be an informative exercise to discover how much a manager knows about coworkers.

It is helpful to know the personal histories and interests of the work force. Some of the best managers may not attempt to discover anything about their workers, but the workers will respond to good managers who take a personal interest in them.

The Work Ethic

Individuals bring their own work ethic to work. The work ethic is the very essence of what a manager must tap into. Operations managers who try to find ways to motivate their workers to increase productivity and quality are given a set of employees with a certain set of work ethics. The work ethic of one region in the world may not be as strong as that of another region, for various cultural or historical reasons.

In February 1992, Kiichi Miyazawa, the prime minister of Japan, commented that Americans did not have as strong a work ethic as the Japanese. Newspaper columnists and television broadcasters in the United States reacted strongly to this statement, some placing this

Table 13–3
Co-worker Familiarity Questionnaire
Fill in the following information about a coworker:

Their name:

Spouse/significant other's name:

Children's names:

Hobbies:

Favorite TV shows:

Their Automobile:

High School/Colleges attended:

Where they grew up:

One previous job:

What motivates them:

What they care about:

"misstatement" on a par with the bombing of Pearl Harbor, another event in which the Japanese awoke the sleeping giant, the United States.

We asked several Americans to share their perspectives on the current state of the American work ethic. Here are their thoughts:

Dr. Joseph Horvath
Compost Scientist
Missoula, Montana

I have complete confidence that America was set aside by God in his eternal wisdom as a refuge for those people all around the world that have been oppressed. I am happy to be a part of this system. I don't know where you stand on God, but I believe America was destined to help the rest of the world. Presently, you can see how without America, the Soviet Union would be in absolute chaos, Eastern Europe would have no hope. The whole world needs that sensitivity and resource that America provides. If you have home, you can advance your camp. Thank God, that's what happened. Interestingly, America doesn't want to rule the world, and it doesn't want to oppress. Those of us who came from outside feel that we can see and appreciate.

The Japanese don't know us at all. Given the opportunity, we can outproduce everybody. Most of the inventions come from here. Most of the thinking and resourcefulness are here. What they have now, America made it possible. We have some lazy people here and there, that's fine, that's normal.

Bob Meyer
Architect
Atlanta, Georgia

I have noticed a difference with the work ethic of the younger people. Maybe I'm just getting old, but when I was getting out of school, I would work on whatever project I could. The other guys in the office in our age group have also noticed the work ethic has changed a little bit.

I'm 36. These kids are like in their early 20s, right out of school with opportunity sitting in front of them, and their mind is basically a void of nothingness. They know enough to be dangerous but not enough to do anything. It's interesting because I've found very few young people coming out of school who realize how little they know. I was overwhelmed when I got out of school. I saw the work they were producing, and I saw what was expected of the young people after a year or two of being there, and I was panicked. I made every effort to listen and learn and get as much exposure to try to understand this monster that was in front of me. I just don't get the same sense. It's a more of a "You owe me. I'm here. I've been here for a year. I deserve to have this responsibility." They have no experience, yet they feel that they deserve it. They've spent time. It's not a question of being qualified. It's a question of the firm owing them that responsibility. It seems like it has changed in the 10 years since I was in the position. Values have changed, and people are putting more priority on their personal time. Which is great, but it pisses me off when I have to spend that much more of my personal time making up because they're enjoying their personal time. If I've got to spend five hours here, I could have spent two hours if I had one or two other people helping in that two hours.

I wish we could say we pay them well enough to say, "Yes, you should be here," but the fact is, we don't. It's not a financial carrot you can hold out to them and say, "You're going to make a lot of money if you stay here and work," because that's not the case. It's just a matter of personal pride in knowing you're doing the best job you possibly can.

One of my friends made a point that a lot of the younger people today, especially ones that come from affluent backgrounds, have never had to work for anything. They didn't have to work to get that first new car. They didn't have to work to get through college. Some of them get out of college and are still living at home. Work is just something to occupy their day, that eight hour segment that starts out the morning. They just don't have the commitment to it because it's not an important part of their life. Pay for that vacation trip. They always have that trust fund or that check from Mom and Dad to fall back on. The people that don't have that are a little more hungry, a little more competitive, have to be little more conscious of every day and that it gets recognized. Unfortunately, it doesn't. That's the sad thing.

If you've got an individual that is just not performing. There may not be anything specific. They may show up on time. They may not leave until the end of the day. They may not take excessive sick days, but they're just not doing the job like you need it done. It's just cruising along, doing the bare minimum, and they're employed for life because you can't get rid of them. In this profession, the deadlines require 150 percent.

John Linke
Entrepreneur
New Orleans, Louisiana

You mentioned that when you were growing up, you worked in a lime plant that influenced your working philosophy.

These were some really nice guys, just solid down-to-the-earth-type guys, but for 35 years they had been roustabouts at this plant. Never any responsibility, just happy doing whatever somebody told them. They might go out and shovel lime away from a railroad track, or they might clean out railway cars or empty coal cars. They were getting into their 60s and still climbing up and sweeping and mopping.

This one old guy, he came in and he had tobacco spit coming down both sides of his face, in the winter. It was cold out there, my feet were freezing, and they liked to give us college kids hell.

He said, "You guys just can't take it. They just don't make them like they used to." You had to bite your tongue sometimes. One guy came around to pick up the dumpsters that we'd filled up from the spills. He said, "Gee, Linke, when I was your age I used to be able to fill eight of those a day. You only filled up three."

I said, "And I'm trying to get down to two. I'm not trying to set any records. Your records are intact as far as I'm concerned." I was not into physical work and just watching these guys that were shoveling for all those years and then listening to them gripe about it, about the heat or the cold, I'd think, "Why don't you do something about this?"

Describe the work ethic of New Orleanians.

Not to be rough on the New Orleanians, but the perception of companies from outside the area was that they wanted someone who liked living in New Orleans who wasn't necessarily from here.

They think that everybody on Friday afternoon goes to lunch, drinks beer, and eats oysters all afternoon and that's it. It's like there's a 4 1/2–day work week. The first day of oyster season, or shrimp season, or duck season, or whatever season is coming in, everybody has a boat or gun and goes and does it. They felt like people are too busy doing the fun things down here and not as intense in their work. Being a midwesterner always made people feel I had a certain work ethic, and I do, but I also believe now, "Hey, it's time to lighten up." Just because you put 40 hours in doesn't mean they're great hours.

Pitt Hesterly
Land Man
Lafayette, Louisiana
What's your perspective of the local work ethic?

Laissez-faire. About five percent of the people do 100 percent of the work. Most come from well-to-do families where they've got a big farm with sugar cane. The money's already been made, so they don't have to do so much. The other extreme is a guy who has to go off shore and work on an oil rig. You can't work as hard here, the weather's so difficult. If you stayed here one summer, you would know. It prevents a full-out effort.

I thought the Japanese prime minister was probably correct. Of course, we don't run sweat shops like they do over there. It's a different philosophy. There's no long-range planning in American corporations.

Phu Nguyen
Technician
Thornton, Colorado
Phu was a young military officer in South Vietnam. After his capture by the North Vietnamese, he spent three years in a relocation camp. After his release, he was sentenced to a life as a farm laborer. Instead, Phu escaped with his family to Hong Kong in a small boat. The second day of the voyage, his wife bore a child on the boat. He has five kids, one at Colorado University.

United States a very good place. A lot of opportunity. I'm not saying 100 percent equal opportunity we have over here. If we work hard, have success. My wife's family has a Chinese restaurant. They work hard, maybe 16 hours a day. They have a Mercedes. My wife's brother, a surgeon, he makes over 100K a year. But he not like it yet. Yale receives him next year. He's young, born in 1957.

If we try hard, we can earn something. At least, we have opportunity.

The Japanese prime minister criticized how hard the Americans work.

How hard do Americans work? It's not like 1945. Now most countries back to normal. United States, like rich. Maybe I the first to come here, I should work hard. Like the first generation from England worked hard. Then the next generation, my daughter and son, work hard, but less. Less than me. My grandchildren, they will say, "Why work hard? Let's enjoy it. We never want for food for hungry. Enjoy every day."

In 1950s, times in U.S. real good. But now, hard. Times are changing.

What's your favorite thing about working here?

> I like the air conditioning to work in. Yeah, not like 100 degrees outside. I'm real lazy when it's 100 degrees. If you comfortable, you work better.
> Sometimes we work hard because we honest. I get paid money to feed my family. I do the job for engineering. They pay for me, I do for them.
> I try to get more education over here. I take English and communications, writing and math. I'm working for a BS in Electrical for myself, not for money. It's my hobby. I don't want to be boring, stay in same job. I like college.

The American work ethic *overall* is alive and well. The Japanese prime minister may have accurately portrayed differences in factory work ethics, for here he has a basis for comparison. However, how does this account for the fact that the United States has the greatest manufacturing productivity in the world? Work ethic differs according to region: we have all heard of the "Protestant" work ethic so predominant in the Midwest. Nancy Vollertsen, in Minnesota, claimed it was too cold to do anything else but work. Meanwhile, in Louisiana, Pitt Hesterly claimed it was too hot to work so hard. So, weather has something to do with it. Obviously, Phu Nguyen did not miss working in the 100-degree heat of Vietnam.

Work ethic differs according to the generation and conditions in which we grew up. Those born in the 1940s and 1950s experienced different environments than those born in the 1970s, and many believe their work ethics are effected by that fact. In any plant or office not driven by a machine pace, work varies, and some people work harder and accomplish more, while others barely get by. This is human nature, and it is often frustrating to the overachievers when reward differentials are minimal. The overachievers know that the managers will look to them to shoulder a greater share of the load. Sometimes they appreciate the responsibility; other times, they resent the intrusion.

Finally, what an operations manager can do about work ethic is search for those people who want to work, set a good personal example, and either change the behavior of the shirkers or find ways to weed them out.

Job Satisfaction

Operations managers across the globe seek the keys to job satisfaction. If they can discover ways to keep the work force satisfied, the work experience can be a much more pleasurable one. Dawis (1992) classified satisfaction reinforcement into six factors:

1. Safety

2. Autonomy
3. Comfort
4. Altruism
5. Achievement
6. Status

Dawis presented 20 reinforcer statements to measure job satisfaction:

1. I could do something that makes use of my abilities.
2. The job would give me a feeling of accomplishment.
3. I could be busy all the time.
4. The job would provide an opportunity for advancement.
5. I could tell people what to do.
6. The company would administer its policies fairly.
7. My pay would compare well with that of other workers.
8. My coworkers would be easy to make friends with.
9. I could try out my own ideas.
10. I could work alone on the job.
11. I could do the work without feeling it is morally wrong.
12. I could get recognition for the work I do.
13. I could make decisions on my own.
14. The job would provide for steady employment.
15. I could do things for other people.
16. I could be "somebody" in the community.
17. My boss would back up the workers.
18. My boss would train the workers well.
19. I could do something different every day.
20. The job would have good working conditions.

(Dawis, R. V., "Person-Environment Fit and Job Satisfaction," in Cranny, C. J., P. C. Smith, and E. F. Stone, *Job Satisfaction*. New York City: Lexington Books, 1992, pp. 69–88.)

Job satisfaction should be periodically measured in the same way customer satisfaction is measured. It is the way managers can take the pulse of their workers and discover if they have any problems brewing. Satisfaction is typically measured using questionnaires administered by the human resource department.

Managers often know intuitively when they have a degree of job satisfaction, but it is still a good idea to take the time to measure it. It is impossible to satisfy all employees, but if the greater majority of them are satisfied, and the customers are buying the products and services, upper management will be satisfied, too.

The Meaning of Work

The *American Heritage Dictionary* defines a job as: "an activity performed for payment, especially one performed regularly as one's occupation." A career is defined as, "a chosen pursuit; lifework." Does a job differ from a career in that it is not something you choose to do, but have to do?

The word "pursuit" is vital to the difference between a job and a career because it connotes a goal. And that is a critical consideration, because to many workers, the only "pursuit" in a job is to get to the end of the day.

The Army's commercial, "It's not just a job!" tells the enlisted man or woman that there is a mission in their work. They are pursuing, working toward, a goal.

Parents stress the importance of jobs almost immediately after an infant child is delivered:

> "Look at those hands! He's definitely going to be a wide receiver!"
> "He looks so serious! I bet he turns out to be a judge!"
> "Look at those eyes! She's a movie star if I ever saw one!"

The comments continue in this vein until a child enters school. If the child seems bright and displays a trait such as a good memory, she will obviously go on to be a doctor/lawyer/professor/engineer, whatever the parents would most like an intelligent daughter to turn out to be. If a boy shows evidence of strong physical development, it's a matter of selecting an athletic endeavor: marathoner/football player/basketball player/gymnast/swimmer. Finally, the child goes off to school to test his or her mettle against other children. Now we begin to separate the wheat from the chaff. The comments take on a new seriousness:

> "You'd better do well in school if you don't want to turn out like your father!"
> "If you don't make good grades, you won't get in a good college, and if you don't get in a good college, you won't get a good job, and if you don't get a good job, you won't find a good wife, and if you don't get a good wife, you won't be happy, and if you're not happy, you'll take it out on our grandchildren and there will never be a doctor in the family!"

Disappointment reigns supreme as many parents discover that their children either don't have the aptitude or the interest in the vocation expected of them. Still, years of education are wasted as students pursue the career their parents wanted them to have and find out, sometimes too late, that they are more suited for something else. Then, there are those rare individuals who know at a young age exactly what they want to do and then go on to do it, love it, and become very successful at it.

In college, the process of selecting a major begins. Many students love the comfort of being "undecided." The pressure continues from their parents,"You'll never get into a better graduate school with these grades!" Cottage industries have sprung up simply to prepare students for such tests as the LSAT, GMAT, and GRE, so that students will achieve scores high enough to gain entrance into the better schools.

A management goal is to have a productive work force, producing quality outputs with limited inputs. But before managers can insist on increased output from their workers, they must have a fundamental understanding on the meaning of work to the individual and to the company. Collectively, these workers take the company where it is going.

One of the greatest challenges of management is to motivate employees who don't perceive themselves as important to the ultimate success or failure of the organization. Somewhere in these employees' lives, they have lost whatever occupational ambitions they may have had as children. Somewhere along the road, these people lost their dreams. Their dreams may have been crushed by the education process, their parents, or the need to make ends meet. The greatest managers are the ones who can revitalize these dreams and reopen possibilities for their workers.

The lower in the organization one manages, the lower the compensation and the lower the aspirations of the employees. Entry-level managers often find themselves with their hardest challenges at the beginning of their careers, because they are managing at this level.

On a busy day on the streets of Manhattan, London, Paris, Atlanta, Hong Kong . . . stop and look at the faces in the crowd. They get up in the morning and work. They are somehow responsible for many things you consume. They save to send their children to college. They write checks when there is no money in the bank. And for 2,000 and more hours a year, they work at a job that greatly determines how they spend their remaining 3,500 waking hours each year.

This, then, is what human-centered production is all about. Recognizing that the faces in the crowd have lives, that they were born with the innate desire to do good work, and that there are ways that they can help a company achieve its goals.

REFERENCES

Dawis, R.V. (1992). "Person-Environment Fit and Job Satisfaction," in C. J. Cranny, P. C. Smith, and E. F. Stone (eds.), *Job Satisfaction*. New York: Lexington Books, pp. 69–88.

Handy, C. (1989). *The Age of Unreason*. Boston: Harvard Business School Press.

Kimberly, J. R. and W. R. Nielsen (1975). "Organizational Development and Change in Organizational Performance." *Administrative Science Quarterly*, 20:196–201.

Lipnack, J. and J. Stamps (1989). *The Team Net Factor*. Essex Junction, TX: Oliver Wight Publications.

Pate, L., W. R. Nielsen, and R. T. Mowday (1977). "A Longitudinal Assessment of the Impact of Organization Development on Absenteeism, Grievance Rates and Product Quality." *Academy of Management Proceedings*, 28:354.

Peters, T. J., and R. H. Waterman, Jr. (1982). *In Search of Excellence*. New York: Warner Books.

Quinn, J. B. (1992). *Intelligent Enterprise*. New York: The Free Press.

Trist, E. L., G. W. Higgin, H. Murray et al. (1963). *Organizational Choice: Capabilities of Groups at the Coal Face Under Changing Technologies*. London: Tavistock.

Wellins, R. S., W. C. Byham, and J. M. Wilson (1991). *Empowered Teams*. San Francisco: Jossey-Bass.

14

Conclusions

This book has focused on the major themes of global operations: the strategic management of operations, the management of quality and productivity, and the service of the human trilogy: employees, customers, and shareholders. These themes have been articulated through a review of the strategic and tactical aspects of global operations. The thoughts of several managers and workers were integrated into the chapters to reveal some of the real issues for today's workers. Many times, we have emphasized that true effectiveness in operations is accomplished through skillful people management and human relations.

Finally, we are left with the question of: "How do you put all this stuff together to succeed at managing across the globe?" Managers often look for the quick-fix approach to deep-seated problems. They want a list of ways to become effective people and a list of methods for managerial excellence. What follows *is* a game plan for success in global operations, with a strong caveat that nothing beats leadership and hard work.

Managers who want to be successful at global operations should heed the following advice:

1. Go native.
2. When in a re-engineering or downsizing mode, make changes thoughtfully and judiciously.
3. It is easier not to build a new plant than it is to close an old plant, and outsourcing can mean never having to say you're sorry.
4. Work at communication and coordination.
5. Empowerment is something to practice, not preach.

6. Quality programs are not short-lived fads. Stick with them.
7. Providing leadership, having technical knowledge, and setting a good personal example are characteristics of the effective global operations manager.
8. Manage underground.

These tips reflect the key themes emphasized throughout this book.

1. Go native.

Whether the assignment is in Paris, Texas; Macon, France; or Hong Kong, the manager must know what the cultural norms are. A storm-trooper approach does not work toward long-term success for a manager. A manager in a foreign environment, such as a Japanese manager in Arkansas or a German manager in England, must be extremely sensitive to what they say, particularly if they are trying to phrase in a foreign tongue.

A manager who enthusiastically experiences local culture becomes more human to his or her employees. If the manager has a genuine distaste for the favorite hobbies of the troops, he or she should have the presence of mind to keep their opinions to themselves. To some people, golf makes as much sense as a tractor pull. Whatever—respect the local interests.

Work is not the place to proselytize a religion or advance political beliefs. Churches and political parties were created for that purpose and have no place in the work place. *At* work, everything should be neutral except for the support of the company. It is a place, in American terms, where Democrats and Republicans must work side-by-side and enjoy each other's company.

2. When in a re-engineering or downsizing mode, make changes thoughtfully and judiciously.

Major process changes, or cuts in the employment size, bring about increased anxiety on the part of the workers. Workers need to be involved in the changes and not left uncertain for long stretches of time. The best way to downsize is to grow smarter. If growth is managed wisely and temporary workers are employed until continued growth is assured, downsizing is less painful. Similarly, there is little need to re-engineer if more thought is put into the creation, purpose, and maintenance of business processes.

3. It is easier not to build a new plant than it is to close an old plant, and outsourcing can mean never having to say you're sorry.

The strategies of how to manage capacity around existing plants often involve decisions on closing plants completely. Companies cannot gain loyalty from their workers if they routinely close existing plants and then open new ones in lower labor-cost markets. Although this is perfectly within their legal rights (usually), it creates an organizational memory that cannot be erased. Because this process is as painful as a personal divorce, once again, it appears much easier to manage growth more carefully than to open and close plants frivolously.

Plants do have a life cycle and many times it makes no economic sense to retool an existing plant with the current technology. Such a situation can usually be predicted several years in advance, and a thoughtful employer will warn the work force of that imminent eventuality, so that they can be the ones who are retooled.

Rather than building a plant, outsourcing should especially be considered where the new capacity cannot be guaranteed long-term. In fast-evolving industries such as the personal computer industry, it may make a lot more sense to contract production. If the increased sales dry up, there is no layoff and no animosity. The contractor, to be sure, loses, but that is a lesson of sub-contracting: never put all of your eggs in one basket.

4. Work at communication and coordination.

Deming's principle of "breaking down the barriers," means that functional areas must increase communication, and make an effort to improve coordination. Coordination mechanisms include joint task forces, joint planning, meetings, and permanent teams.

In some companies, distrust has developed across departments, and a preliminary step in breaking the barriers is to ensure trust. Managers with specialized training are not prepared for the sometime human tragedy we call work. All of the expertise in inventory and scheduling techniques can be quickly eroded by human power struggles.

Although it is easy to say that all of the factions should resolve their differences, shake hands, and work together to accomplish organizational goals, that is not the way that it works. We recommended (in an earlier chapter) the practice of functional job rotation for managers. An organizational awareness of the need for coordination is also necessary. New managers must be set straight in their orientation periods. To break old patterns, organizational consultants may be the answer.

5. Empowerment is something to practice, not preach.

Next to TQM seminars, the most popular management seminars in the 1990s have been on the subject of empowerment. These seminars have failed, for the most part, to change those that don't feel workers can be trusted with empowerment.

Many managers are incapable of empowering their workers, because they want control, and feel that they will lose value and stature if they relinquish power. What do we do about these managers? If the Chief Executive Officer truly believes in this principle, then maybe the Theory X–type managers should be screened out at the job interview stage. Another solution might be to channel these people into staff positions, where at least they have control over their own computer and calculator.

It may be that the process of empowering goes against much of our cultural upbringing. After all, as children we were controlled by our parents, and as parents we controlled our children. Very few children are given the option of deciding their bedtime, curfew, and whether they can have the car on a Saturday night. We are used to controlling, and being controlled.

The message is: "If letting go of control is uncomfortable, work on it until it becomes comfortable."

6. Quality programs are not short-lived fads. Stick with them.

Total quality management programs require a commitment of blood, sweat, and tears for several years before an organizational transformation can happen. Many managers give up on these programs, especially if the results are meager in the initial months. Granted, it is difficult to introduce new work while existing chores must get done, but it is a price that must be paid today to reap rewards tomorrow.

Probably the first aspect of TQM to be forsaken is the data-gathering aspect. Some managers may embrace the empowerment concepts of TQM, and that is a necessary ingredient, but without data, there is no evidence of improvement.

TQM must be accepted as a fact of life, something you are in for the long haul. Managers who give it short shrift do not have the long-term best interests of the company at heart.

7. Providing leadership, having technical knowledge, and setting a good personal example are characteristics of the effective global operations manager.

In many companies, more employees work in the operations function than in any other area of the firm. Often, operations managers are dependent on some of the lowest-paid workers in the firm. Operations managers who want to rally the troops, motivate them, and get them to outperform their expectations, must provide leadership.

Some operations managers are more attracted to the technical side of management than the people side. Finding new ways to schedule machines, new algorithms for materials scheduling, or designing new assembly lines can be more exciting to an operations manager than settling a wage dispute, developing an incentive pay system, or counseling a unit that is underperforming.

Technical knowledge is something that a good operations manager attains through learning. Some operations managers may have an engineering education, and this aptitude comes in handy with the technological demands of production. However, it is not an absolute necessity for the operations manager to come to the company with this knowledge. It is doubtful the operations manager will ever have to disassemble machinery, although it is nice to know what makes it run.

Henry Ford is generally regarded as a production genius. Yet, he once went to court to sue a writer who claimed he was mentally incompetent. In the court case, Ford's argument was that all he needed to know was who to ask for advice. If he pushed one button, he could get an accounting expert. Another button led to a financial expert. The knack of knowing who to ask is really all the less-than-technically-minded individual needs. A truly thorough manager stays on top of technology and has a passable literacy when talking to the real technical experts.

8. Manage underground.

The lesson from the Turris Mine in Illinois is to work at the trench level with the workers. Respected managers do not stay in the air-conditioned comforts of their office while problems develop and go unsolved on the floor. Walking around and stopping, observing, discussing, and promising action are what the best managers do.

A manager cannot fake interest in an employee or an employee's work. There must be a genuine concern for employees, who must be provided the tools they need to do the job right. Managers who have worked their way up the organization have the benefit of knowing more about what goes on at the various levels of the company.

Managers who work in foreign countries must find ways to relate to the work force, and their knowledge of how the work gets done is a minimal requirement to their success. Line supervisors and workers do not care for senior managers who are out of touch with what they are doing. If this means spending a day flipping water buffalo burgers in Zimbabwe, that is what the manager must do.

A form of managing underground is knowing the customers. Effective managers understand the needs and wants of the customer, and will go to great lengths to make sure they are well served.

In summary, what global operations is all about is managing people effectively to accomplish the transformation of raw materials or customers into high quality goods and services. Much of the science of operations management concerns the application of various heuristics, formulas, and equations to solve production problems, and those numerical approaches are well covered in introductory production and operations management texts. The emphasis here is on the big themes of global operations, so that managers can ponder the bigger picture before getting down to the detailed tactics of production management.

Production and operations management academics have always been plagued with a situation in which practice is leading theory. Practitioners develop new operations methods, for example, JIT, and then the academics analyze them, compare them with other methods, and go off to analyze an infinite combination of possible scenarios, while the practitioners have already moved on to developing even newer methods. The lack of having a laboratory, an experimental setting in which to test theories, handicaps the researcher. Businesses do not allow theorists to come in and tamper with their existing systems, thus simulation models are developed to study "what-if" scenarios. Production management is still a discipline in need of qualitative field research. One approach we have used to understand operations problems is simply to talk to the rank and file, and some of their comments are printed here. It is the rank and file who drive production success, and we cannot reduce their variability to a simple equation.

An intention of this book has been to discuss the state of the art of today's operations management, while reviewing the many problem areas and offering potential solutions to the problems managers face. Ultimately, the success of the global operations manager will be directly proportional to effort, motivation, involvement, and the people of the workforce.

Bibliography

Adler, N. J. "Pacific Basin Managers: A Gaijin, Not a Woman." *Women in Management Worldwide*. (N. J. Adler and D. N. Izraeli, eds.). New York: M.E. Sharpe Inc., 1988, pp. 226–249.

Adler, N. J. and D. N. Izraeli. "Women in Management Worldwide." *Women in Management Worldwide*. (N. J. Adler and D. N. Izraeli, eds.). New York: M. E. Sharpe Inc., 1988, pp. 3–16.

Adler, N. J. *International Dimensions of Organizational Behavior*. 2nd ed. Belmont, CA: Wadsworth Publishing, 1991.

Albrecht, K. and R. Zemke. *Service America: Doing Business in the New Economy*. Homewood, IL: Dow Jones-Irwin, 1985.

Angelidis, J. *Countertrade* (Unpublished dissertation). Atlanta: Georgia State University, 1989.

Axtell, R. *Do's and Taboos Around the World*. 3rd ed. New York: John Wiley & Sons, 1993.

Badiru, A. B. *Expert Systems Applications in Engineering and Manufacturing*. Englewood Cliffs, NJ: Prentice-Hall, 1992.

Barras, R. "Towards a Theory of Innovation in Services." *Research Policy*, 15:161–173, 1986.

Bartlett, C. A. and S. Ghoshal. *Managing Across Borders: The Transnational Solution*. Boston: Harvard Business School Press, 1989.

"The Best Cities for Knowledge Workers." *Fortune*, November 15, 1993, pp. 50–78.

Bowman, R. J. "Quality Management Comes to Global Transportation." *World Trade*, 6(2):38–40, 1993.

Boyer, R. and D. Savageau. *Places Rated Almanac*, Englewood Cliffs, NJ: Prentice-Hall, 1989, 1993.

"Brace for Japan's Hot New Strategy." *Fortune*, September 21, 1992, pp. 61–74.

Brandeau, M. and S. S. Chiu. "An Overview of Representative Problems." *Management Science*, 35(6):645–674, 1989.

Bibliography

Bureau of Business Practice. *Profile of ISO 9000*. Needham Heights, MA: Allyn & Bacon, 1992.

Burgess, A. R. and J. B. Killebrew. "Variation in Activity Level on a Cyclical Arrow Diagram." *Journal of Industrial Engineering* 13(2):76–83, 1962.

Burroughs, B. and J. Helyar. *Barbarians at the Gate*. New York: Harper & Row, 1990.

BusinessWeek, August 31, 1992, p. 29.

Charnes, A., W. W. Cooper, and E. Rhodes. "Evaluating Program and Managerial Efficiency: An Application of Data Envelope Analysis to Program Follow-Through." *Management Science*, 27:668–697, 1981.

Chase, R. B. "The Customer Contact Approach to Services: Theoretical Bases and Practical Extension." *Operations Research*, 29(4):698–706, 1981.

Chase, R. and N. Aquilano. *Production and Operations Management*. Homewood, IL: Irwin, 1992.

Cherrington, D. J. *The Management of Human Resources*. Boston: Allyn & Bacon, 1991.

"Citicorp Chief Reed, Once A Big Thinker, Gets Down to Basics," *Wall Street Journal*, June 25, 1993, pp. 1, 4.

Clark, T. B. and A. P. Young. *Project Management with the Critical Path Method*. Atlanta: Young, Clark and Associates, 1985.

Collier, D. A. "The Service Sector Revolution: The Automation of Services." *Long Range Planning*, 16(6):10–20, 1983.

Commission of the European Communities. *The Social Aspects of Technological Developments Relating to the European Machine-Tool Industry*. Luxembourg: Office for Official Publications of the European Communities, 1986.

Czinkota, M. R. P., P. Rivoli, and I. A. Ronkainen. *International Business* (2nd ed.). Fort Worth: The Dryden Press, 1992.

Daniels, P. W. *Service Industries in the World Economy*. Oxford, United Kingdom: Blackwell, 1993.

Davenport, A. "Forging a Modern Machine Tool Industry." *The China Business Review*, May-June, 1988, pp. 38–44.

Davidow, W. H. and B. Uttal. "Service Companies: Focus or Falter." *Harvard Business Review*, 6(4):77–85, 1989.

Dawis, R. V. "Person-Environment Fit and Job Satisfaction." *Job Satisfaction*. (Cranny, C. J., P. C. Smith, and E. F. Stone, eds.) New York: Lexington Books, 1992, pp. 69–88.

de Meyer, A. and K. Ferdows. "Integration of Information Systems in Manufacturing," *International Journal of Operations and Production Management*, 5:5–12, 1985.

Deming, W. E. *Out of the Crisis*. Cambridge, MA: MIT Press, 1982.

Dun & Bradstreet, Canada, Ltd. *Canadian Book of Corporate Management*. Toronto: Dun & Bradstreet, 1980.

Elfring, T. "New Evidence on the Expansion of Service Employment in Advanced Economies." *The Service Industries Journal*, 9:337–356, 1989.

Engen, J. R. "Getting Your Chinese Workforce Up to Speed." *International Business*, 7(8):44–48, 1994.

Fallows, J. M. *More Like Us: Making America Great Again*. Boston: Houghton-Mifflin, 1989.

Ferdows, K., J. G. Miller, J. Nakane et al. "Evolving Global Manufacturing Strategies: Projections into the 1990s," *International Journal of Operations and Production Management*, 6(4):5–14, 1985.

Fimstahl, T. W. "My Employees are my Service Guarantee." *Harvard Business Review*, 67(4):28–32, 1989.

Forger, G. "Making Bar Code Labels and EDI Pay Off." *Modern Materials Handling*, 46(7):57–59, 1991.

Forger, G. "Warehouse Upgrade Records a 30% Efficiency Gain." *Modern Materials Handling*, 48(10):38–40, 1993.

Galbraith, J. R. *Designing Complex Organizations*. Reading, MA: Addison-Wesley Publishing Company, 1993.

Garnier, G. "The Autonomy of Foreign Subsidiaries: Environmental and National Influences." *Journal of General Management*, 10(1):57–82, 1984.

Garvin, D. A. *Operations Strategy*. Englewood Cliffs, NJ: Prentice-Hall, 1992.

Garvin, D. A. "Quality Problems, Policies, and Attitudes in the United States and Japan: An Exploratory Study." *Academy of Management Journal*, 29:653–673, 1986.

Ghadar, F., W. Davidson, and C. Feigenoff. *U.S. Industrial Competitiveness*. Lexington, MA: Lexington Books, 1987.

"GM Drive to Step Up Efficiency is Colliding with UAW Job Fears." *Wall Street Journal*, June 23, 1993, pp. 1, 8.

Gonenc, R. "Changing Economics of International Trade in Services." (B. R. Guile and J. B. Quinn, eds.), *Technology in Services*. Washington, DC: National Academy Press, 1988, pp. 167–186.

Hammer, M. and J. Champy, *Reengineering the Corporation*. New York: Harper Business, 1993.

Hamper, B. *Rivethead*. New York: Warner Books, 1986.

Handy, C. *The Age of Unreason*. Boston: Harvard Business School Press, 1989.

Harrington, H. J. *Business Process Improvement*, New York: McGraw-Hill, 1991.

Hart, C. W. L., J. L. Heskett, and W. E. Sasser, Jr. "The Profitable Art of Service Recovery." *Harvard Business Review*, 68(4):148–56, 1990.

Hart, C. W. L. "The Power of Unconditional Service Guarantees." *Harvard Business Review*, 66(4): 54–62, 1988.

Hayes, R. H., Wheelwright, S. C., and Clark, K. B. *Dynamic Manufacturing*. New York: The Free Press, 1988.

Hayes, R. H., and W. J. Abernathy. "Managing Our Way to Economic Decline." *Harvard Business Review*, Vol. 58:67–77, Jul./Aug. 1980.

Hayes, R. H. and S. C. Wheelwright. *Restoring our Competitive Edge*. New York: John Wiley & Sons, 1984.

Haywood, B., and J. Bessant. "Organisation and Integration of Production Systems." *New Technology and Manufacturing Management*. (M. Warner, W. Wobbe, and P. Brodner, eds.), Chichester, West Sussex, United Kingdom: John Wiley & Sons, 1990.

Henkoff, R. "The Hot New Seal of Quality." *Fortune*, June 28, 1993, pp. 116–120.

Herbert, T. T. "Strategy and Multinational Organization Structure: An Interorganizational Relationships Perspective." *Academy of Management Review*, 9(92):259–270, 1989.

Herzberg, F., B. Mausner, and B. Snyderman. *The Motivation to Work*. (2nd ed.). New York: Wiley, 1959.

Hofstede, G. *Culture's Consequences*. Beverly Hills: Sage Publications, 1980.

"Holding the Lead in the Machine Tool Industry Proves Tough." 1987. *Business Japan*, 32:95–104.

Holland, M. *When the Machine Stopped*. Boston: Harvard Business School Press, 1989.

Horsley, J. P. "The Chinese Workforce." *The China Business Review*, May-June: 50–55, 1988.

Hrebiniak, L. G. and W. F. Joyce. *Implementing Strategy*. New York: Macmillan Publishing Co., 1984.

Juran, J. M., F. M. Gryna, Jr., and R. S. Bingham, Jr. (eds.), *Quality Control Handbook*. New York: McGraw-Hill, 1988.

Kang, T. W. *Is Korea the Next Japan?* New York: The Free Press, 1989.

Kimberly, J. R., and W. R. Nielsen. "Organizational Development and Change in Organizational Performance." *Administrative Science Quarterly*, 20:196–201, 1975.

Kimes, S. E. and J. A. Fitzsimmons. "Selecting Profitable Hotel Sites at La Quinta Motor Inns." *Interfaces*, 20(2):12–20, 1990.

Kirkpatrick, D. "Groupware Goes Boom." *Fortune*, December 27, 1993, pp. 99–104.

Kluckhohn, C. "Values and Value-Orientations in the Theory of Action: An Exploration in Definition and Classification." (T. Parsons and E. A. Shils, eds.) *Towards a General Theory of Action*. Cambridge, MA: Harvard University Press, 1951.

Kohn, A. "Why Incentive Plans Cannot Work." *Harvard Business Review*, 71(5):54–63, 1993.

Kroeber, A. and C. Kluckhohn. *A Critical Review of Concepts and Definitions*. New York: Random House, 1985.

Lawrence, P. R. and J. W. Lorsch. *Organization and Environment*. Boston, MA: Harvard University Graduate School of Business Administration, 1967.

Leap, T. L. and M. D. Crino. *Personnel/Human Resource Management*. New York: Macmillan, 1989.

Lipnack, J. and Stamps, J. *The Team Net Factor*. Essex Junction, TX: Oliver Wight Publications, 1989.

Maister, D. "The Psychology of Waiting Lines." *The Service Encounter*. (J.A. Czepiel, M.R. Solomon, and C.F. Surprenant, eds.), Lexington, MA: Lexington Books, D.C. Heath and Company, 1985.

Majchrzak, A. *The Human Side of Factory Automation*. San Francisco: Jossey-Bass, 1988.

"Mapping For Dollars." *Fortune*, October 18, 1993, pp. 91–96.

Martinez, J. T. and J. C. Jarillo. "The Evolution of Research on Coordination Mechanisms in Multinational Corporations." *Journal of International Business Studies*, Fall: 489–514, 1989.

Miller, J. G., A. De Meyer, and J. Nakane. *Benchmarking Global Manufacturing*. Homewood, IL: Business One Irwin, 1992.

Mosher, P., and A. Majchrzak. "Workplace Changes Mediating Effect of Technology on Individuals' Attitudes and Performance." Presented at the Academy of Management. Chicago, 1986.

Myrdal, G. *Asian Drama: An Inquiry into the Poverty of Nations.* New York: Pantheon, 1971, pp. 39.

Ouchi, W. *Theory Z.* New York: Addison-Wesley, 1981.

Pate, L., W.R. Nielsen, and R.T. Mowday. "A Longitudinal Assessment of the Impact of Organization Development on Absenteeism, Grievance Rates and Product Quality." *Academy of Management Proceedings,* Vol. 37:354, 1977.

Peters, T. J., and R. H. Waterman, Jr. *In Search of Excellence.* New York: Warner Books, 1982.

Porter, M. E. *Competition in Global Industries.* Boston, MA: The Free Press, 1986.

Porter, M. E. *The Competitive Advantage of Nations.* New York: The Free Press, 1990.

Porter, M. E. *Competitive Advantage.* New York: The Free Press, 1985.

Quinn, J. B. *Intelligent Enterprise.* New York: The Free Press, 1992.

Quinn, J. B. "Technology in Services: Past Myths and Future Challenges." *Technology in Services* (B.R. Guile and J.B. Quinn, eds.). Washington, D.C.: National Academy Press, 1988, pp. 16–46.

Reichheld, F. F. and W. E. Sasser, Jr. "Zero Defections: Quality Comes to Services." *Harvard Business Review,* 68(5):105–111, 1990.

Render, B., and J. Heizer. *Principles of Operations Management.* Boston: Allyn & Bacon, 1994.

Rho, B. and D. C. Whybark. "Comparing Manufacturing Practices in the People's Republic of China and South Korea." Working Paper No. 4. Indiana University: Indiana Center for Global Business, 1988.

Ricks, D. A. *Big Business Blunders.* Homewood, IL: Irwin, 1983.

Ruben, B. D. "Guidelines for Cross-Cultural Communication Effectiveness." *Group and Organization Studies,* 2: 470–479, 1977.

Sarathy, R. "The Interplay of Industrial Policy and nternational Strategy: Japan's Machine Tool Industry." *California Management Review,* 31(3): 132–160, 1989.

Savageau, D., and R. Boyer. *Places Rated Almanac,* Englewood Cliffs, NJ: Prentice-Hall, 1994.

Schmenner, R. W. *Production/Operations Management* (3rd ed). New York: Macmillan Publishing Co., 1993.

Schonberger, R. J. *Japanese Manufacturing Techniques.* New York: The Free Press, 1982.

Schroeder, R. *Operations Management: Decision Making in the Operations Function* (3rd ed). New York: McGraw-Hill, 1993.

Shapiro, B. P. "Can Marketing and Manufacturing Coexist?" *Harvard Business Review,* 55(5):104–114, 1977 (Reprint No. 77511).

Sherman, H. D. "Improving the Productivity of Service Businesses." *Sloan Management Review,* 25:11–23, 1984.

Sheth, J. and G. Eshghi. *Global Operations Perspectives.* Cincinnati: South-Western Publishing, 1992.

Sink, D. S. *Productivity Management: Planning, Measurement and Evaluation Control and Improvement.* New York: John Wiley & Sons, 1985.

Skinner, W. *Manufacturing in the Corporate Strategy.* New York: John Wiley & Sons, 1978.

Slevin, D. P. and J. K. Pinto. "Balancing Strategy and Tactics in Project Implementation." *Sloan Management Review,* Fall: 33–41, 1987.

Standard & Poors Industry Surveys. New York: Standard & Poors, 1990.

Tan, A. "Women Urged to Take High-Tech Road." *The Straits Times,* November, 1984, pp.19.

Terpstra, V. and K. David. *The Cultural Environment of International Business.* Cincinnati: South-Western Publishing, 1981.

Thamhain, H. J. and D. L. Wilemon. "Criteria for Controlling Projects According to Plan." *Project Management Journal,* June: 75–81, 1986.

Thompson, J. P. *Organizations in Action.* New York: McGraw-Hill Book Company, 1967.

Toledano, S. H. "Mexican Location Considerations." *Business Mexico,* 3(4):11–14, 1993.

Toyne, B., J. Arpan, A. Barnett. *The Global Textile Industry.* London: George Allen & Unwin, 1984.

Trist, E. L., G. W. Higgin, H. Murray et al. *Organizational Choice: Capabilities of Groups at the Coal Face Under Changing Technologies.* London: Tavistock, 1963.

Tsjovold, D. "Cooperative and Competitive Interdependence." *Group and Organization Studies.* 13(3):275–289, 1989.

"Volvo's Radical New Plant: 'The Death of the Assembly Line.'" *BusinessWeek,* August 28, 1989, pp. 92–94.

Wellins, R. S., W. C. Byham, and J. M. Wilson. *Empowered Teams.* San Francisco: Jossey-Bass, 1991.

"Why Mercedes is Alabama Bound." *BusinessWeek,* October 11, 1993, pp.138–139.

Wobbe, W. "A European View of Advanced Manufacturing in the United States." *New Technology and Manufacturing Management.* (Warner, M., Wobbe, W., and P. Brodner, eds.) Chichester, West Sussex, United Kingdom: John Wiley & Sons, 1990.

The World Bank. *Korea: Managing the Industrial Transition.* Washington, DC: The World Bank, 1987.

World Christian Encyclopedia. Oxford University Press, 1983.

Young, S. T. and W. Nie. "A Cycle Count Model Considering Inventory Policy and Record Variance." *Production and Inventory Management Journal,* First Quarter, pp.11–16, 1992.

Young, S. T. "Multiple Productivity Measurement Approaches for Management." *Health Care Management Review,* 17(2):57–58, 1992.

Zeithaml, V. A., A. Parasuraman, and L.L. Berry. *Delivering Quality Service.* New York: The Free Press, 1990.

Zhuang, S. C. and A. M. Whitehill. "Will China Adopt Western Management Practices?" *Business Horizons,* March-April: 58–64, 1989.

Index

ABOUT THE AUTHORS

SCOTT T. YOUNG is Chair and Associate Professor of the Management Department at the David Eccles School of Business at the University of Utah. Dr. Young has researched and published extensively in the areas of global operations, service operations, productivity, and quality.

WINTER NIE is Assistant Professor in the Management Department at Colorado State University. Dr. Nie researches and teaches in international operations management and service operations.